Galactic Healing

To Rachel

Also by Shelley Kaehr, Ph.D.

Books:

Origins of Huna: Secret Behind the Secret Science
Gemstone Journeys
Lifestream: Journey into Past & Future Lives
Beyond Reality: Evidence of Parallel Universes
Edgar Cayce's Guide to Gemstones, Minerals, Metals & More
Divination of God: Ancient Tool of Prophecy Revealed
Just Write It: Step By Step Guide to Writing & Publishing Your First Book
Lemurian Seeds: Hope For Humanity

Videos:

Gemstone Journeys
Stones of Power

CD's:

Galactic Healing: Healing with the Elements
Origins of Huna: Ho-oponopono Cord-Cutting
Lifestream
Journey to Spirit: Meeting Your Guides
Journey to Spirit: Abundance
Sacred Sounds
Journey to Grief Recovery

Order online at www.galactichealing.org

FIRST EDITION
First Printing, 2003

Edited by Cheryl Doyle
Cover design by Shelley Kaehr
Photo of Buzz Aldrin © NASA

Library of Congress Control Number: 2003095656

Kaehr, Shelley A., 1967-
          Galactic healing /
Shelley Kaehr - 1st ed.
p. cm.
Includes bibliographical references.
ISBN: 0-9719340-4-5

An Out of This World Production does not have any authority concerning private business transactions between our authors and the public. If you wish to contact the author or would like more information about this book, please write to the author in care of An Out of This World Production and we will forward your request. Please write to:

Shelley Kaehr, Ph.D.
 c/o An Out of This World Production
P.O. Box 610943
Dallas, TX 75261-0943

www.outofthisworldpublishing.com

Galactic Healing

Shelley Kaehr, Ph.D.

To
The Universe

and all of the wonderful people who made this work possible including: Mickey, Gail and Mark Kaehr, Joe Crosson, Cheryl Doyle, Martha Switzer, and all of my friends and clients...

THANK YOU!!

Table of Contents
Introduction

Fundamentals of Energy Work

The Galactic Healing Process

Humans are very peculiar.
I often find them unfathomable,
but an interesting
psychological study.

Mr. Spock

One

Before we begin our discussion of Galactic Healing, I want to share some background information with you. If you read my first book, *Origins of Huna: Secret Behind the Secret Science*, I mentioned a near-death experience I had several years ago and briefly discussed that, after that experience, I seemed to instantly acquire healing abilities I did not know I had before. Because timing was not right and the context of that book was not an appropriate place to disclose all that went on during that event, I am now prepared to tell what happened on that strange evening that forever changed my life.

13

I want to share that experience with you again in greater detail and describe how it ultimately led me to develop the Galactic Healing System.

At the time, I was living in Colorado and was planning a trip with a small group to South Africa, a place that had been "calling" to me for quite awhile. Unfortunately, the trip was suddenly cancelled and my friend and I decided we might as well take a month and go somewhere, since we had already set aside the time and money to take a trip.

"Where would you want to go if you could go anywhere in the world?" he asked.

"Egypt!" I said, hardly drawing into consciousness the fact that it was the middle of summer there.

"Where do you want to go?"

"Turkey!" he said.

So we decided to go to those two places and make Greece our central spot on the tour. I had also been wanting to go to Greece since childhood, so we decided to fly into Athens and go on from there to the other destinations.

Like most of my trips, I had absolutely no itinerary. I remember when we first got to Athens how wonderful it was to me. I remember putting my feet in the sea and feeling the energy from the pebbles that had crashed upon that shore for hundreds, maybe thousands of years. It was really amazing. More amazing to me, though, was this feeling I had that surpassed any sense of déjà vu I had ever known. This place seemed so familiar to me and yet I had never been there before as far as I could recall in this lifetime. My feet had definitely been on that beach before. I was sure of it. It felt like more than just a past life connection, though, as I stared up at the whitewashed dwellings on the cliffs all around me. It was as if I knew exactly where everything was and that I knew all was exactly as it should be. I had been to this place. *This place.* Exactly as it was in modern times. It was a strange feeling. Had I astral traveled there? I had no idea, I only knew that I loved it.

The entire trip changed my life. We began in Athens and explored Delphi, and the ruins of the Oracles of the Dead and then flew to Cairo, exploring the pyramids and the Valley of the Kings and other temples and Egyptian monuments. That story is something in and of itself I am sure to save for another time.

Then we returned to Greece and spent some time in Rhodes before taking a boat over to Turkey. We drove up the West coast visiting the lost city of Troy, and Ephasus - the home of the Virgin Mary, and ended up in Istanbul for a visit to the huge market you may have seen on TV where they sell all of the wonderful Turkish rugs. We eventually ended the trip back in Athens. It was an amazing journey!

When I returned to Denver five weeks later, I was not the same person. It would take me months and even years to realize just how significant the trip had actually been.

Two

The two weeks after my return from
Greece were strange. I began to feel despondent
and depressed. I felt lower than I ever had in my
life. I began questioning my mortality and wondered if I even wanted to stay on the planet at all. I
wondered if I was feeling a postponed bout of
depression over my divorce six months earlier.

Looking back, I now doubt that was the
case at all. There was really much more going on
than I could've imagined.

In one of the most important books in
Christian Mysticism by St. John of the Cross called
Dark Night of the Soul, the author explains these
dark nights are times when God shuts your soul off

from all worldly pleasures in order to cause you to receive a spiritual boost.

According to St. John:
"When a soul finds no pleasure or consolation in the things of God, it also fails to find it in anything created; for as God sets the soul in this dark night to the end that He may quench and purge its sensual desire, He allows it not to find attraction or sweetness in anything whatsoever."

Was God trying to cut me off from the world to turn up the volume on my spiritual nature for some grander purpose? Perhaps.

Others who have heard my story speculate I may be a walk-in, like those in Ruth Montgomery's classic book *Strangers Among Us*.

More recently, Doreen Virtue described walk-ins as a type of earth angel in her book *Healing With the Angels*:

The walk-in is a highly evolved spiritual being with a light worker life purpose... needed to incarnate in a hurry...and decided to bypass the usual method of developing as a fetus, being born, and growing up...the walk-in soul located

*a living human who was not happy being alive
... then communicated, usually through dreams
or thought-transfer, to the depressed person and
said "I will take over your responsibilities for
you , and you will be able to go home without
any negative repercussions associated with
suicide. "*

According to Virtue, the walk-in goes
through a drastic personality and lifestyle change
and close friends and relatives sometimes have
trouble relating to this new personality in the old
shell as the new soul may choose to change habits
and routines or even their name.

My own dark night of the soul occurred just
a few weeks after my return from Greece. One
afternoon I "heard" my guides tell me there was
something wrong with my heart and I would not live
much longer. That evening my heart slowed to a
near stop and I found myself floating inside the
tunnel of white light described by Dr. Raymond
Moody in his classic bestseller *Life After Life*. The
tunnel of light was the most beautiful and peaceful
place I had ever experienced. It is impossible to
describe. While there, I met my deceased grand-
mother and my aunt and I knew this was a serious
situation!

Obviously, I survived, and then spent the next two weeks occasionally feeling myself slipping out of my body into a space between life and death. I wondered for awhile if I was going to live, but eventually that passed.

I would love to say here that things went back to normal, but actually after that experience, I was never the same again.

Since that time, I have talked to dozens of people who experienced near-death situations and all say it changed them for the better. Was I a walk-in, was this my dark night of the soul, or did that brush with the infinite light of God change my personality and outlook forever? I still don't know the answer. Months later, I would receive yet another possible explanation for this profound transformation.

It was during this time, as I mentioned earlier, I realized I had a gift for healing. If you read my other works, you know I believe we are all gifted with the ability to heal ourselves and others. I believe this gift is often dormant within us because we may have done this in other lifetimes and may have forgotten how to do it in this life. Sometimes we need a dramatic life changing experience to help us remember, as I apparently did.

Shortly after my trip in the white light tunnel,

I began doing healing work on myself at night before I went to sleep. I would place my hand on parts of my body and run powerful energy to them. I was intuitively told that I would be doing hands-on healing for others someday. At the time, I found the thought to be totally ridiculous.

The experience led me on a journey to discover more about this gift and how to use it and I began to study all types of healing modalities - Reiki, Huna, gemstones, healing touch, polarity, you name it, I took a look at it.

During the time I began to write *Origins of Huna*, I somehow created a portal in my home where many unseen friends were constantly coming through to give information to me.

By a portal, I mean it was like a doorway to the other side that had been created in an up-stairs room in my home. This made it easier for spirits to come through there. Because of the direct communication pathway created in the room, I began a series of automatic writings from many guides. Through these writings, I learned I was to name my spiritual healing practice Galactic Healing and I would have a healing modality I would share with the world by the same name.

Soon afterward, I began to channel star symbols and performed extremely advanced healings and what I would describe as exorcisms on people who had what some call spirit attachments. Many indigenous cultures believe, as I do, that sometimes people can display strange behavior or mental illness caused by a wandering spirit attaching itself to the person's auric field. The process of exorcism is done to remove this unwanted energy from the person's energy field so they may become healthy and whole again. I was doing quite a lot of this work at this time and I must say, it was extremely interesting. I was fortunate to be led to the right books and helped by the right guides - many native American and Hawaiian shamans, who taught me how to perform these tasks.

During this time, I was intuitively introduced to a third explanation for my near-death experience. I was told by many people to read the book *Bringers of the Dawn* by Barbara Marciniak. At first, I ignored the message until so many people began telling me to get it, I knew it had to be more than a coincidence and I finally bought the book and read it.

At the beginning of the book, Marciniak describes her trip to Athens, Greece, and the fact that it was there she began channeling the Pleiadians, good-willed beings from the star system of the Seven Sisters.

What stunned me was that the story she tells in the book seemed so similar to my own - the places she visited in both Greece and Egypt and the life altering events that occurred for her upon her return. During her trip there, Marciniak says she was contacted by Pleiadians who began to channel important planetary messages to her. In the book she gives her conclusion that Athens, Greece, is the portal on Earth through which the Pleiadians have come to help us.

I was told that I, too, had somehow contacted these high beings during my trip to Athens. The trip into the light tunnel had allowed me to remember lost parts of myself and a soul contract I had to complete in this lifetime - to eventually bring healing galactic energies to earth and share the star symbols with the help of my extraterrestrial guides.

I was told these symbols would help humanity by providing total healing and restoration to those who had a deep commitment to using the technology.

In the book *Quantum Healing* by Deepak Chopra, the author describes the etheric double and the fact that this "blueprint" of our body is actually representative of how we are in perfect health. It is a blueprint of perfection.

Since the human body completely regenerates itself, cell by cell, every seven years, the question I have always asked is why do we continue to regenerate the same heart problem or bum leg, or whatever?

I believe the answer lies in the fact that humans have yet to remember how to fully connect with our blueprint of perfection. If we could somehow learn how to bridge the gap between what we are now with our energetic blockages, aches and pains, to the total perfection of our bodies as they were intended to be, we could heal anything. We could regenerate bad organs, clean our blood, eliminate cancers and viruses and live happy and healthy lives.

Let me repeat that: *I believe we can heal ourselves totally from head to toe!*

My guides told me the Galactic Healing system will be a major part of that process.

What if we could tap into that perfection right now? At this point, this may sound a little far fetched and 'way out' to you, but over the years, and despite even my own doubts, I have seen miracle after miracle using this energy and I am a total believer in it!

Before we get started, I want to tell you I totally respect and honor all forms of energy healing. There is no "one way" to do anything, so in these pages I will offer you this information as another tool to use to connect you to your Source of the divine fire within.

Every single modality has its place in the world and different frequencies benefit everyone in different ways. We are all part of the vast universe in which we live. Each modality serves as a pipeline to connect us with our creator.

The processes contained in these pages are the most powerful connection to Source I have found yet. Perhaps you will find the same. This is just one way to bring through the energy, and if you find yourself reading this book, I would suggest that there is at least a part of you that resonates to the contents.

So keep an open mind and remember: if you can take even one thing out of this book to actually put to use in your life to make life happier, easier and better for yourself, then it was time well spent. It is my sincere hope to make our time together of value for you. So what are you waiting for? Let's begin!

Fundamentals
of Energy Work

Three
The Chakras

First, it is important to understand some basic fundamentals before we get into the actual healing processes.

What is energy work?

I get this question all the time and it is one I used to ask myself. The best way I know to describe this is to share an analogy. Have you ever had a massage? I'm not necessarily talking about a professional massage -just a back rub from a friend, or someone squeezing your shoulders when they are tight. The person massaging you is attempting to bring some form of balance back to your physical body by touching it, right? Energy work is like that except instead of working with your physical body, the practitioner works with the energetic part of you - your soul - and works the kinks and blockages out of your energy field so you can achieve optimal health.

In my book *Gemstone Journeys*, I discuss energy fields and portals, or energetic pathways around the body, at length. As you move through life, this energetic part of you gets a bit blocked at times. It is called *stress*, and your ability to handle or not handle the naturally occurring stresses in life is part of what you come here to learn.

The energetic part of you is something you may not have considered before. A good example of this is if you have ever been to a funeral. When I go to a funeral, I find myself gazing into the casket, looking down on my friend or loved one and thinking "That's strange! Bob's body is there, but *he* is not there!"

That is the big question of life-where did "Bob" go? The energetic component, or soul, has gone somewhere else. While we are on the earth plane it is important to realize this energetic part of us is real and must be cared for.

The reason I became interested in this work

is because when I was ill several years ago, some-body said to me, "You're in such bad shape you need energy work!"

My reply was, "What's that?" I had never heard of it before, and since then, I have used all sorts of methods to totally transform my health and every other part of my life.

I believe it is critical to teach people about the energetic, or spiritual, nature of themselves because it is from the spiritual level that people will heal and can totally transform their lives.

As a Galactic Healing practitioner, I hope you will share my passion for spreading the word to others about the importance of caring for and maintaining the spiritual part of ourselves. It can literally change someone's life, and you can be a big part of helping people live happier, healthier lives by simply teaching them about energy and how it affects you.

First, it will be important to understand one of the basic concepts of energy healing work which you will learn in the next section - the chakras.

The Seven Chakras

According to Eastern esoteric thought, the chakras are energy centers in the human body that correspond to seven colors in the rainbow spectrum. In other words, these centers, when they are open and properly functioning, are vibrating at the same speed as different colors of light. If we were actually able to see the chakras, they would look like colored tornadoes, beginning at the base of the spine and working up to the top of the head.

Root

The root, or first, chakra is located at the base of the spine and vibrates to the color red. When functioning properly, this chakra keeps us grounded in earthly activities, and helps us feel centered and connected to the earth. If we are feeling "spaced out," confused, or disconnected from reality, there may be a blockage there. In eastern thought, the root is the location of the kundalini energy that resides at the base of the spine and eventually leads us to enlightenment. It is also one of the chakra centers that allows us to manifest on the physical plane.

Chapter Three

Sacral

The sacral, or second, chakra vibrates to the orange color frequency and is located just below the navel. It is the seat of creation -the part of you that is able to create and manifest. Combined with the root chakra, it is the primary source for our creative energies. The second chakra is also our sexual center.

The healthy functioning of the first and second chakras combined enables us to not only create, but to actually finish things and bring them out on the physical plane. An example of someone with a well-functioning second chakra is an artist who produces a painting and takes it to an art show to sell.

Solar Plexus

The third chakra, or solar plexus, is located at the convergence of the ribcage.

It vibrates to the color yellow and is the seat of our personal power.

How we stand up for ourselves and demonstrate courage are the lessons of the solar plexus chakra.

The Chakras

Crown

Third Eye

Throat

Heart

Solar Plexus

Sacral

Root

Heart

The fourth chakra is the heart. It surprises many people that the heart chakra vibrates to the color green, since we often associate it with rosy red or pink. While these colors are also very healing to our hearts, it is actually the healing green of Mother Nature herself that best resonates with our heart center.

Since heart disease is still the number one killer in the United States and other nations, it will be interesting to observe the changes that will occur over our lifetimes as we successfully shift our attention to love and away from greedy materialism. Lessons of the heart deal not only with loving others, but with loving ourselves as well - not an easy journey for many of us.

Throat

The fifth, or throat, chakra is light blue and is all about communication. By "communication," I mean how we speak our truth in the world. As we are able to accept ourselves more and to share our ideas and personal truth as we see it, we open our throat chakras.

It is interesting to notice in yourself and others when you may have a little tickle in your throat or begin to have a cough and you know you are not ill. A lot of times, this can mean you need to say something to someone that is difficult. This is a tough lesson for all of us, potentially because so many of us have suffered persecution in past lives as a result of our beliefs.

Conscious effort to open this center can really pay off in the long run because the tension from not expressing our truth can eventually become quite a burden on the body.

Third Eye

The third eye is the sixth chakra, located on the forehead. This is our mystical, psychic, intuitive center, and the one chakra many of us would most like to open. The third eye chakra vibrates to the color of indigo, a purplish blue. Many times in spiritual work you may see a purple light inside your head. This happens quite a bit with my hypnosis clients. Sometimes what they are experiencing is the opening of the intuitive center of themselves, since much of the hypnotic work is done using their own intuition. Pay attention next time you notice a purple light. It could be a sign you are opening up!

Crown

The seventh, or crown, chakra connects us to God. As its name suggests, it is located at the top of your head, and it vibrates to the colors white or violet. Deep meditation and visualization of connecting with Father Sky, the stars, and the heavens can facilitate the opening of the crown. The crown is the place in all of us where all universal and divine love is downloaded into our being.

In addition to the seven chakras we discussed earlier, there are literally hundreds of other minor energetic centers that correspond not only to the physical body, but to the energetic body. You will learn more about these in a later chapter.

In my opinion, having a good working knowledge of the seven basic centers is key to success in healing. Usually if you can work to open each one of the primary seven centers, the client will feel infinitely better, since most major illnesses correspond to one of these centers.

The following pages list some common illnesses and the chakra center that corresponds to each.

Use this and all information in this book as a guideline to help you in healing, but do your best to avoid relying on it entirely.

I want you to get more used to relying on your own inner voice and intuition.

Your guides and guardian angels will always help you to know what is best in any given situation.

Pay attention to that source of knowledge above all!

Chakras & Corresponding Illnesses

The following list shows possible illnesses that could occur when chakras are either under or over active. This is not meant to replace medical attention or advice, but should be used as a guide to prevent illness altogether.

ROOT

hemorrhoids
constipation
irritable bowel
bladder problems
eating disorders
anorexia
bulimia
weight disorders

SACRAL

reproductive disorders
diarrhea
appendix
impotence
endometriosis
fibroid tumors

SOLAR PLEXUS   stomach problems
liver
gallbladder
pancreas
spleen
kidney

HEART   heart attack
congenital heart failure
high blood pressure
lung problems
weak lung capacity
addictions

THROAT   endocrine, gland system
asthma
bronchitis
pneumonia
sore throat
tonsillitis
mumps
thyroid imbalance

THIRD EYE

headache
migraine
eye problems
macular degeneration
astigmatism
inflexibility
vertigo/dizziness

CROWN

headache
depression
lack of motivation
brain tumors
aneurysm
schizophrenia
autism

Four

The Subtle Energy System

In addition to the chakra centers, there are three energetic layers around the physical body: astral, mental, and causal, known as the subtle energy system, or the spiritual bodies.

These energetic bodies are your direct link with your creator and everything else in the universe.

One of the goals of energy work is to remove blockages from the spiritual bodies so you may be more perfectly connected to Source.

Spiritual Energetic Bodies

When your spiritual bodies are fully functioning, your energy field has the potential to emanate over 25 feet around your physical body.

The challenge we face in our lifetimes is to be able to deal with stress in such a way as to not allow it to interfere with the maximum potential of our energy field.

There is literally no telling what you are capable of when your energy is working at full capacity. You have unlimited potential. Releasing the spiritual bodies from blockages will assist you in achieving and being all you can possibly be in your lifetime.

Each layer of your spirit deals with different parts of your existence. Understanding them can help you on your path.

The first layer deals in more earthly work while the others move gradually off into more spiritual realms.

We will review each one of them briefly here because understanding the concept of the spiritual bodies will be an important part of your healing work regardless of the modality you are using.

Chapter Four

Astral

The astral body is the energetic layer closest to your physical body. It is the place we speak of when we describe "astral traveling" and it is where you may often go in the dream state to meet with other souls or to work on more mundane tasks.

A good analogy for the astral is that it is like doing work around the house, or paying your bills. Not the most spiritual work around by most standards, however, it is necessary to do in order to function in the world.

When we are working on our energetic layers, it is important to concentrate on removing blockages from this layer first because it is only a few inches away from the physical body. Blockages that have a chance to reach the physical body are most likely to cause illness.

When I work with clients for the first time, I may spend the first session or two just working to remove the energetic blockages in this layer. On subsequent visits, we can then be free to work on the higher levels.

Once this layer is clear, the client can move into healing the other layers dealing with different levels of learning and soul development.

Mental

On most people I have encountered, the mental body is the layer of energy that is about six to eight inches beyond the physical body.

We manifest and create from the mental body, and the energy here allows abundance to flow to us. Creative endeavors such as writing, painting or music are also manifested in the mental body. Blockages in the mental body literally block our creativity and hinder our ability to attract abundance.

While the astral is about doing household chores, the mental body would be like nourishing our minds by taking classes or reading books. It is a step up on the spiritual ladder, so to speak.

Any creative endeavor is a wonderful expression of your soul's divine potential and ability to manifest your God-given talents on the physical plane. That is the function of the mental body.

Causal

The causal, or spiritual, body is the part of you that is connected to the life force, or God. This is the spiritual self - the soul.

If the astral is like your worldly duties and the mental is your education, the causal is your connection to God, or your spiritual work. This could mean your meditation practices, your prayers and your soul contracts.

I believe that all illnesses begin out in the causal body and vibrate inward toward the physical body.

Some illness may be brought on by day-to-day stresses, such as work, relationship or financial challenges.

Other illness is brought on by karma, in other words, I believe we are born with it and it is built in to our system at specific times to help teach us lessons we came here to learn.

I briefly mentioned earlier about how I first got interested in alternative medicine after suffering a very long chronic and painful illness, prior to my near-death experience. I believe that illness happened at a specific time and for a specific reason to help me get to the point where I am today, to a place where I feel I can really understand and help other people. That situation, in my opinion, was part of my karma, or soul contract for certain lessons it was to teach me.

Energy work gives us the gift of being able to clear karmic blockages in our minds without having to undergo the trauma of serious illness.

That is not to say it will treat every illness.

Perhaps you cannot learn a lesson unless it is played out fully in the third dimension.

For me, I can say this was certainly the case. I did not even know what energy work was at the time of my own illness. I do believe the total manifestation of that situation ultimately served a greater good that could not have been achieved as well if the blockages had been removed prematurely. I needed to get the learning in the way I did for a reason.

You may have soul contracts of your own that were first created in the causal body, or you may know of people who have. Haven't you ever noticed when something really bizarre happens to someone - too coincidental to be a coincidence, so to speak?

A friend of mine recently went to the dentist to have an abscessed tooth fixed. Shortly after having the dental work, in a bizzare turn of events, he developed a horrible infection in his arm. Three days later, he tragically had to have it amputated.

He is one of the bravest and most humble souls I know. When I spoke to him shortly after the accident, he told me he knew this situation was "scheduled" in the divine plan for him to learn from. That is one of the best examples of understanding a soul contract I have ever encountered.

Spiritual Energetic Bodies

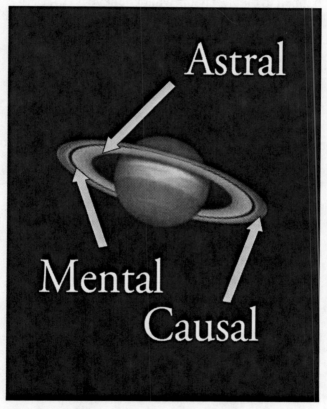

This illustration of Saturn's rings looks similar to what your spiritual bodies would look like around your body if you could see them.

There are times, though, I have found that people do not have to go through all the things that happen to them. That is what I believe is part of my mission here: to help others understand their life lessons without as much trauma as I had and without having to "crash and burn."

Understanding we are all responsible for things we are experiencing here is very powerful in that it helps us to learn to create what we want, instead of what we do not want.

For me, it also helps to explain the injustices in life and the fact that things just are what they are and that all things really do have purpose and reason. We may not like some of these things, but they all serve a purpose in teaching us and allowing our souls to evolve.

So to conclude, it is very important to understand the energetic bodies and the role they play in connecting us all to our source of knowledge and wisdom. For it is through that source that we will evolve into conscious beings.

Five

Higher Dimensions

Before we can move on, we need to discuss a very important concept that will shape your understanding of the rest of this information - the existence of other dimensions of reality.

It has been well established by the scientific community that other higher planes of existence actually do exist.

There is a lot of speculation amongst new age thinkers about the nature of the fourth dimension and other higher planes of consciousness. Lots of people have theories, as I do, as to what the nature of these upper dimensions really are, but the truth is, that just like all of the other great mysteries, I believe we will not ever really know for sure until we cross over into the afterlife.

The fourth dimension, and really any dimension that is of a higher frequency than we are currently existing in, is really difficult for us to understand with our third dimensional minds. I believe you can understand it at a soul level more than in an actual conscious mind level.

One of the best examples of how difficult it would be to explain other dimensions is in a fascinating book written in the 1800's called *Flatland* by Edwin A. Abbott. In the book, Abbott describes a society living in a two dimensional world and the challenges faced by beings who cannot perceive three dimensions. Abbott's narrator, A. Square, shows us how to perceive the world through the eyes of a Flatlander, who is living in the second dimension:

"Place a penny on one of your tables in space; and leaning over it, look down upon it. It will appear a circle.

But now, drawing back to the edge of the table, gradually lower your eyes (thus bringing

yourself more and more into the condition of the
inhabitants of Flatland), and you will find the
penny becoming more and more oval to your
view; and at last when you have placed your eye
exactly on the edge of the table (so that you are,
as it were, actually a Flatlander) the penny will
then have ceased to appear oval at all, and will
have become, so far as you can see, a straight
line."

Flatlander, p. 7-8

So as you can see, in the second dimension,
everything appears like a flat line with no shape.
The inhabitants of such a world would have an
awfully hard time imagining what it would be like to
live as we do in a world of three dimensional depth.

The narrator in the book is the only person
around who can perceive the higher, third dimension
and he is met with ridicule and an inability to
describe his experience to the people of Flatland:

"I - alas, I alone in Flatland - know now only
too well the true solution to this mysterious
problem; but my knowledge cannot be made
intelligible to a single one of my countrymen;
and I am mocked at - I, the sole possessor of the

truths of space and of the theory of the introduc-
tion of Light from the world of Three Dimen-
sions - as if I were the maddest of the mad!"

Flatlander p. 11

Does this sound familiar? I am sure there
are plenty of people who have experienced other
realms of consciousness and told friends and
colleagues about them only to be laughed out of the
room. This has happened to me on a few occasions! You may know what I'm talking about!

So the difficulty in describing each one of
the dimensions I am about to mention is a given. I
am not inclined to speculate about the nature of
various dimensions I do not know anything about. I
will tell you about my own limited perception of a
vast and complex subject.

The fourth dimension, in my understanding,
is a space where time is non-existent. In our world,
everything is linear and we view time as if today is
now, there is a past filled usually with things we
regret, and a future filled with hope and promise.

Unfortunately, most of us are incredibly
preoccupied with living either in the past or the
future. We often find ourselves dwelling on and
reminiscing about past events, or living solely for

some future event that will totally transform us and relieve us of our current perceived misery and misfortune.

The truth is, physicists are now speculating that there is no such thing as time. All things are now. We can think about this concept in our minds, yet to really get a handle on all of the possible ramifications of such thinking is really tough to do.

What does that mean - *all time is now*? Could all events actually be happening all at once, somewhere on some other dimension? I believe they are.

In my private practice I take people through past and future memory journeys. How can I possibly guide someone to journey, not only to places in the past, but to places in the future? If everything is actually happening all at once on some other plane of existence, then I believe it is possible to access those other realms while we are in a hypnotic state.

It never ceases to amaze me that nearly every person I have worked with, let's say 90% of all people who come in to see me, actually have some sort of experience either through pictures, sounds or feelings, concerning some other time period where their soul has existed or will exist.

It is an amazing process for me to witness and I feel very honored to be able to be present with people as they make the most amazing discoveries about themselves. I am merely the "tour guide to the unconscious mind," because it is the client who is really doing all the work of pulling up the memories and soul insights.

People occassionally ask me if past- life regression is valid, and I really don't have a definite answer for that. I have found this information is deeply imbedded in the subconscious minds of the people I work with and therefore has some meaning to them, be it actual or symbolic. Therefore, I really don't care if it is "real" or not as long as the understanding of the information is of some value to the person when they are through.

Yes, of course I believe we have lived before, yet that is not what is really important. It is of greater priority that the people feel better and come to understand themselves and their lives more deeply than before.

Have you ever wondered how psychics work? How are they able to go into trance and pull up things about your future, and then later, you discover those things actually happen? They are looking into another dimension, in my opinion.

The thing is, you can do this yourself if you

have a little practice. Although we all know it is tough to see things going on in your own life objectively without going to a third party, so it can be a good idea to consult someone from time to time. I want to make sure you know, though, you can actually do this yourself! You have all the power and knowledge already stored within you. It's just a matter of learning to tap into it.

So what would it feel like to live in a place where linear time does not exist and all things happen simultaneously? It is hard to imagine, but I think it would mean that we would be able to manifest and create things instantly just by thinking about them.

In energy healing, any time you use any modality of healing or vibrational medicine such as a gemstone you are attempting to create a bridge between your physical self and your energetic self, as we discussed earlier. By doing that, I have personally found the act of manifestation becomes easier and easier as time goes on.

The same would be said of meditation. You have heard over and over again how powerful meditation can be in assisting us to tap into higher planes of consciousness so our manifestation process becomes almost instant.

Deepak Chopra describes this space as

"the gap" the space where all is possible. I think this is similar to what we are talking about here - the fourth dimension. If you read Deepak's book called *The Seven Spiritual Laws of Success*, that is what it is talking about.

Aside from deep meditation, you can also achieve this state of connectedness to higher dimensions by simply having these higher chakra centers activated.

I had a wonderful example of this working for me recently. I needed to buy a new car before going out on a long tour. I thought one day briefly about how I did not have time to go get a car and that unless it was very easy, I would have to put it off until I returned from the trip three and a half months later.

I briefly thought about what car I would want and I imagined one of the new Volkswagon Beetles in my mind. I thought, "If I could have any car right now, that would be the one!"

Amazingly a week later, the neighbors across the street from my house decided to sell their Bug. It had been on a lease and was three years old with incredibly low mileage on it, in impeccable condition. As soon as I saw it, I bought it on the spot! Could it be any easier than that? All I had to do was cross the street and I got exactly what I had envisioned.

That is a simple example of the power of connecting to the forth dimension, in my opinion.

You can do this too! Although right now it may seem hard to imagine being able to think about something and have it show up instantly, but it is definitely possible!

The caution here is to be careful because you will get exactly what you ask for. That is something I learned in my classes in neuro-linguistic programming some years ago. Your mind is just like a computer. - what you put in comes out. Your programming must be checked and updated to ensure the output reflects the input. Sometimes our input is not always the best, so we need to check it and make proper adjustments to ensure success. Particularly in the fourth dimension, you will get what you ask for right away.

Once I was unloading my car and I put the keys on the seat while I moved a heavy box. I thought, "If I don't move the keys now, I will lock them inside the car." The next thing I knew, I had slammed the car door and the keys were still inside. I had not done that in years, yet I really manifested it well.

Another time I went to Houston to teach a gem healing class. I put one of my favorite sweatshirts ont he bed and thought, "If I don't move that, I will leave it here." Sure enough, that is exactly what I did.

Am I just absent minded, or am I manifesting exactly what I asked for? I prefer to think the latter!

Another interesting point is that your unconscious mind does not understand that you are separate from other people. When you call someone "Beautiful," or "Stupid," your subconscious cannot tell the difference between you and the person you are talking about. We are all connected, so be kind to yourself by being kind to others.

I am not going to speculate the nature of any other dimensions for this writing. The bottom line is that the Galactic Healing system is going to connect you with five etheric chakras above the crown of your head.

We will take a closer look at this concept in the next chapter.

Six

Etheric Chakra System

If I was to tell you the difference between Galactic Healing and other modalities I have used through the years, I would say that the Galactic works more on the etheric, spiritual bodies than on the physical.

The elements, which you will learn later in the book, deal more with the physical body while Galactic Frequency is working on the energetic layers of your spirit that connect you with your source. Specifically, Galactic Healing activates parts of what I call your Etheric Chakra System.

This chapter will tell you all you will need to know, for now, about the Etheric Chakra System, which lies beyond your physical body.

In the previous chapters, you learned about the seven primary chakras within your physical body, and I briefly mentioned that there are literally hundreds, if not thousands, of other minor energy centers known as meridian lines all throughout your body.

You also learned about the spiritual bodies - the astral, mental and causal. These are the three main spiritual layers that surround you, yet your energetic field is literally infinite. That is a pretty mind-boggling concept to think about. When you hear somebody say, "We are all connected," it's true! Your etheric energy system cannot be seen by the naked eye, yet it connects you with everything in the universe.

One of the main purposes of the Galactic Healing system is to activate a lesser-known chakra system that lies within the energetic part of you. Some call it an inner planetary chakra system, I choose to call it the Etheric Chakra System.

Because we are infinite, I am sure your etheric body has millions of other chakra centers, but for purposes of this work, I want you to think of the Etheric Chakra System that we will discuss here as being the main ones, kind of like the other seven chakras are to your physical body.

There are five etheric chakras that will be activated for you when you complete level four of the Galactic Healing program. These five are located in the energy field above your head, above your crown chakra. They are:

Silver- the first etheric chakra lies six inches above your head and connects you with the fourth dimension

Gold - the second lies about twelve inches above your head and connects you with the fifth dimension

Copper - the third etheric chakra lies eighteen inches above your head and connects you with the sixth dimension

Platinum - the fourth etheric chakra which is two feet above the top of your head connects you with the seventh dimension. It has golden pink undertones.

Opalescent - this chakra is the fifth and looks like a bluish tinted opal or moonstone and connects you with the eighth dimension. It is about two and half feet above your head.

I asked my guides why we need to be connected with the higher dimensions if we can't even understand the fourth dimension. There are many new age thinkers who believe that the planet Earth is undergoing massive energetic frequency shifts at the present time and that it is our mission while here to raise our vibrational levels up high enough to be able to soon function in a fourth dimensional reality. If that is true, then why bother with the rest of the dimensions and attempting to connect with them if our only goal in our lifetime is to raise to the fourth?

Here is what I was told. I was given an analogy to share with you. Have you ever been camping in a tent? I'm not talking about those great new dome ones because they require absolutely no work to put up. I'm talking about the old ones that used to have stakes and ropes holding them up.

If you were to go pitch a tent in the old fashioned way, you would first lay it out on the ground and it would be flat. We can imagine that this flat tent represents how we are in the third dimension consciousness.

We need some assistance to get us up to the fourth dimension and that comes through the aid of stakes and ropes. The ropes are attached to the tent and then pulled as far away from the tent as possible and held down with a stake. Then after

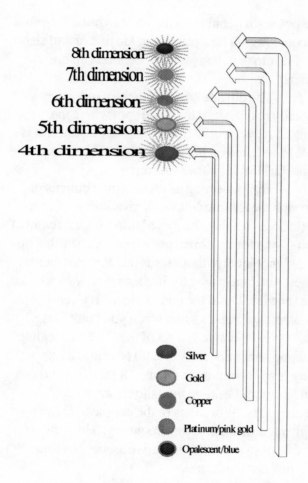

8th dimension
7th dimension
6th dimension
5th dimension
4th dimension

Silver
Gold
Copper
Platinum/pink gold
Opalescent/blue

The Etheric Chakra System

the poles are put in the tent, you can hoist it up so it becomes a 3-D tent you can get inside of and sleep in. Prior to that, it is just like a blanket on the ground.

The outside edges of the tent will never actually reach out to the same spot where the stakes are, yet it is because of them that the tent is able to be lifted up in the first place. This process in Galactic Healing is the same thing.

By connecting us to our higher dimensions through the Etheric Chakra Activation, your energetic body is able to be pulled into a higher realm of being - the fourth dimension. It cannot be lifted up to a higher level without some support from somewhere and that is why the higher activations are like the ropes that hold the tent in place. It is really amazing and makes sense when you think of it.

In level five and six of the Galactic Healing training, practitioners will learn how to activate these upper chakras in clients. It may be used as a very powerful healing modality, in an of itself, to help raise the vibrations of the people here to a higher fourth dimensional frequency. This will enable us to live here and thrive as we move into the new consciousness.

There is also a lot of talk now about the special children being born at this time called

Indigos. You can read the book *The Indigo Children* by Lee Carroll and Jan Tober. I talked to Jan personally about them and she says these kids are born with an indigo colored aura and have different DNA than we do.

I believe they are coming in to our world now fully able to function in the fourth dimensional reality. The problem is that most of them are really young kids right now, and so meanwhile we need adults who can assist in the accession of the planet. That is why the energetic activation is so important to us older folks. We do not have the luxury of twenty years it will take our kids to reach adulthood to make the changes necessary to save the planet. We have to get on to that right now. There is no time to wait.

On to other characteristics of these five Etheric Chakra centers: they each form a loop that goes all the way around your body and comes out your feet. You can see this clearly on the diagram I have included in the book.

Later in the book you will see why this concept is critical to your understanding of Galactic Healing and the entire modality.

Seven

Healing Ethics

Next we will discuss some of the most controversial and debated aspects of healing - ethics. I will share some of the most commonly asked questions concerning this topic.

Can I give somebody too much energy?

This is a question I also hear a lot and I have two stories to share with you that best illustrate my answer to this question.

When I was developing as a Reiki practitioner, I would often go to a 'Reiki Share' where Reiki
students could meet and exchange ideas, techniques, and give healing to each other. You may
have been to a gathering like this before.

Once when I was there, the group was
insistent on limiting the time we could give each
other treatments because they were afraid we
would give people "too much energy."

When you become a healer, you will begin
to notice when you step into a room that, on
occasion, your hands will become hot, which I
interpret to mean that somebody in the room needs
healing. I just ask that the healing go to whomever
needs it, and often I do not even try to tune in to
who that is, I just let it be.

I volunteered for some time at a hospice,
which is a care unit for the terminally ill. I would
visit dying patients in their homes and read to them,
offer companionship or do whatever else I could to
help them and their families. During this experience,
I discovered something really interesting.

Whenever I would go to see one of my
"angels," as we would call them, my hands would
not get hot, no matter what. Of course, I did not
want my hands to get hot because I was not there
to "heal" them - not physically, that is. As an

experiment, one day I concentrated on sending energy to one of my angels just to see what would happen, and found that it was absolutely impossible for my hands to heat up. Now why do you suppose that is?

It is because in hospice care, the client is in a state of what is called "actively dying." They are no longer attempting to sustain themselves, and they are preparing for the other side. The role of the hospice worker is not to "heal" people physically, but to help in the emotional healing process of letting go. Death is a part of the life cycle and it is part of what we agreed to when we got here. It is impossible to use healing touch on people who are actively dying because they do not want healing.

To make this point clearer to you, what I am saying is this:

You cannot heal anyone, at anytime without their permission at least on an unconscious level. Period.

On that note, I want to discuss the "ethics" of healing as I see it. This is one of the most debated and controversial subjects of any healing work and throughout the years, I have developed my own thoughts on the subject.

Again, I offer a story. I was hosting a radio

talk show when a woman called in and told me her son was dying and she wanted my help. I could hear the desperation in her voice as she explained that he was suffering from severe throat cancer and had an inoperable tumor. She wanted to know if I could come see him.

Based on the details of the conversation, I felt that she did not have his permission to do this, so I told her I would not come out unless she actually talked to him and he agreed to see me.

A few days later, she called and said he was ready and willing so I came over to the house. When I walked in, it was obvious he was in severe pain and the tumor was blocking his windpipe so his breathing was laborious. I introduced myself and asked him, "Do you really want to do this, because I respect your wishes and want you to feel totally comfortable with the process. I believe in miracles, that any situation can be turned around if you want it to be. I also believe in your right to choose whether or not this is your time to go and, if so, I honor that too."

He said yes, he was ready and willing to heal. This is what he told me with his conscious mind - out of his mouth as his mother watched. As soon as I began my work, I closed my eyes and his image popped into my mind. In my mind's eye, he

looked healthy like I think he would've looked
before the cancer.

     I said, "Hello. What can I do for you?"

     He said, "I don't really want to do this. I'm
just doing it for my mom."

     I said, "Okay. I totally understand and
respect that. Would you allow me to help you
today to ease your pain and help you breathe easier
so you can be more comfortable?'

     "Okay," he said, and it was then, and only
then, that the energy started to flow from my hands.

     Shortly after that session and one more I
did, again with pain relief in mind, he passed away.
During this time, I worked with the mother to help
her let go and heal from his death.

     We all have to ultimately understand that in
life, no matter how much we want to save people
and keep them with us, in the end it is their choice
alone as to when it is time to live, and when it is
time to die. So to tell you again: you can never heal
anyone without their permission on some level.

     Hypnosis is the same way. People are
often afraid of being hypnotized, fearing they will
somehow be subconsciously subjected to "mind
control." That is total nonsense. Nothing is further
from the truth. You cannot be hypnotized unless
you want to be, and under hypnosis, you will *never*

ever do anything that would jeopardize your safety and take you out of the bounds of what you are willing to do at an unconscious level. Meaning, those people who "flap their wings like birds" on stage, are probably just fun loving people who don't mind getting a few laughs out of people. Otherwise, they would never do it!

In summary, you are completely in charge of your own unconscious mind at all times, and you and your client are responsible, at least at an unconscious level, for how much energy will be exchanged. That is a function of the higher self. You have the power, so claim it!

Other Guidelines for Doing Energy Work

As a new Galactic Healing practitioner, there are several other things to remember that will make your healing practice successful:

1) Before beginning any session, wash your hands.

2) Bring a white light around yourself and those you work on. Say aloud or to yourself: " Only that which is of love and light may enter here."
3) Before you transfer energy, bring your hands to

prayer position and say a silent or spoken prayer to God/Spirit/Source for the well-being of the client. It could sound something like this: "Dear God, I ask for healing and transformation of (person's name) today. I ask that higher will be done."

4) Allow the person to accept or reject this healing by saying either aloud or to yourself: "You are free to accept or reject this healing." This addresses the ethics of healing we talked about earlier.

5) When the healing is finished, again bring your hands to prayer position and repeat a prayer such as: "May higher will be done. Allow this healing to continue." And again see the person bathed in a sealed off white ball of light. Visualize or feel that the client is totally healed and in perfect health and spirits.

6) After the session, you may want to bathe in a salt bath of preferably sea salts or Epsom salts. Salt cleanses your aura of other's energies. (more on salt later in the book) If taking a bath is not convenient, you should spritz yourself with essential oils or flower essences that also work to cleanse you.

Eight

Emotional Clearing

Having slain anger, one sleeps soundly;
Having slain anger, one does not sorrow;
The killing of anger,
With its poisoned root and honeyed tip:
This is the killing the noble ones praise,
For having slain that, one does not sorrow.

Buddha

When I describe the possibility of totally restoring our bodies to perfection, I do not want to mislead you by making this process sound as simple as waving a wand. As I said earlier, this gift is available to anyone. If you have the commitment and willingness to take a non-judgmental look at yourself and be ready to totally heal and transform your life and soul at all levels, read on.

One of the major considerations of this concept is karma. Karma is the spiritual idea of "as above, so below," or "what you put out is what you get back." I believe we have lived in many different lifetimes and our souls come here through the ages to experience all kinds of things in order to learn lessons. People whom society deem as "good" or "evil," under this philosophy, are neither. They just are what they are and come to play that particular role in the development of humanity. In the end, we are all part of the same one Source so when I begin now to talk about karma, I am not speaking of hellfire and brimstone, but rather the vehicle in which we come here to learn about ourselves and others.

I believe it would be impossible to be born into this life totally healed and perfect because it is through our illnesses that we learn, grow, and work out our karma here on the earth plane.

In my private practice, many of the illnesses I have worked with stem from past lives and old energy patterns we are unconsciously holding onto. I believe it is our lesson when we get here to wake up, realize this is old stuff, and somehow figure out how to move beyond it. Fortunately, while it is not easy to do so, it is not as hard as it looks either.

The first part of the process you'll be doing helps you to clear karmic blockages and restore balance to your soul.

Level one of the program involves the elements and your ability to command the forces of nature within yourself and the world around you. By command, I am not talking about some sort of "control." I mean that by the end of this level of training, you will be a master of balance in your own body. You will easily recognizing when you are out of the flow and know how to regain stability easily and effortlessly with the help of spirit and the elemental forces.

Only when you are in balance can you truly help another, so it is important to use these techniques first on self and then on others.

There is a saying that our bodies are microcosms of everything in the universe, so you can feel in your body where there is "dis-ease" and discomfort. By becoming aware of your own discomfort and working to heal it, you are actually healing everyone in the universe!

I remember a time years ago when I forgot what it was like to feel good. You may know what I am talking about. Again and again, people come into my office with the same problem. They hardly know how to heal because they are so used to feeling bad. Many cannot even recall a time when they felt at peace.

So the first step to healing is becoming aware that there is something to heal! Sounds silly, doesn't it? But it's true.

When you can master your own energy and become consciously aware of when you are out of balance, you will be far ahead of most of the population. One of the reasons you may have decided to become a healer yourself could be that you feel an inner calling to help your brothers and sisters on earth. The first step again, is by helping yourself first. Then you can show others how.

Negative emotions cause imbalance, and often, no matter how much healing you do with people in your current life, things may still come up that cause you to wonder if you've done any work on yourself at all. People's emotions are like onions and we just keep peeling back the layers of old patterns and emotional blocks until we eventually get to the core of who we really are - children of God and the universe. I believe most people who become healers are very old souls and these negative emotions are often rooted deeply in our past lives.

I remember years ago when I first began doing a lot of healing and releasing of negative emotions. I was regressed to a point at the beginning of time when I was just a ball of light and connected to Source. Healing at that level provides a very deep realignment of emotions that will shift your soul back into a state of love.

Love is the only real emotion. Everything else is just a form of the opposite of love. You have probably heard this before, and it's true.

You create everything in your life through your perceptions of the world. If you believe you are afraid, you create situations that manifest scary things into your life. On the other hand, if you feel you are blessed, or "lucky" then you will create situations that reflect that back to you as well.

You may have seen the movie the *Matrix* and the *Matrix Reloaded*. In the first movie, Neo is working in a humdrum job that he hates, going through the motions of life, when he is contacted and pulled out of the Matrix - an intricate computer program. He wakes up and sees that everything he once thought was real was only in his mind.

Both movies explore his adventures and the way he claims his power by realizing that everything he gets is exactly what he creates. He becomes a master of his own destiny. He cannot be killed, he cannot be intimidated by things he once feared, and he can do amazing things like flying and blocking bullets with his own self generated energy fields.

I want to tell you that in your life, you are the ultimate master of your destiny as well! You can do and create anything you want, anything you desire. So wouldn't it be great to create what you really want - a life filled with love and joy and peace?

In the *Course In Miracles*, the main point of the book is that everything we see is an illusion that we create ourselves. Wouldn't it be great to make that illusion as positive and healing as possible? If hell is what we create in our minds with the illusions of fear and hatred, releasing negative emotions and learning to forgive will enable us to create the best world possible. In fact, the *Course* states that the only reason why forgiveness is so important to us is because it is the tool we use to rid ourselves of these negative emotions of fear, anger and guilt. These are all self-imposed illusions we have created that we need to overcome in our lifetime.

I was asked recently to write an article on the meaning of Grace and how it can be applied to our lives. I think it is an appropriate concept to look at as we begin the process of healing our past. Webster's New World Dictionary defines Grace as:

"A sense of what is right and proper; decency, thoughtfulness toward others, good will, favor, a period of time granted beyond the date set for the performance of an act or the payment of an obligation, the unmerited love and favor of God toward man."

If God can grant, "unmerited love" to us, then why is it so difficult for us to grant love to each other and to ourselves?

To me, Grace is forgiveness. It is the ability to rise above judgment and hurt feelings and look upon others as souls, realizing we are all part of one another.

People are usually doing the very best they can, so when someone does something that upsets us, we should look at it as part of what that person came here to teach us and realize the intent is not usually malicious. Then we can eventually attain peace within ourselves.

Grace is also *"the period of time granted beyond the date set for the performance of an act or payment of an obligation."*

There is a story in Matthew 25: 15-24 about God granting talents to three men. He gave one of them one talent, another two talents and the other five talents. After a period of reasonable time, he returned to check to see what they had done with their talents. The man with five talents took them and turned them into ten, the man with two turned them to four and the one with only one talent took it and buried it in the earth for fear of losing it and for that, God was angry and took it from him and gave it to the man with ten talents.

Grace can be granted, yet after a reasonable time, it is okay to be upset when reasonable progress is not made. This is part of the learning process we come here for. I believe we meet people for a reason and they are in our lives to teach us lessons.

Just as it is a good practice to give people a chance and extend grace, it is just as good a lesson to know when enough is enough and move on. It is a reflection of our own boundaries and learning to love ourselves enough to say 'when' and move on when a relationship or situation is not serving us any more and *know that is okay*!

My personal challenge and the one I pose to you today is to consider extending grace to yourself and others in your life. See if you can consciously rise above the duality mentality and remember we are all one. Most importantly, remember to extend grace to yourself! We are perfect in God's eyes. Before we can spread grace we must grant it to ourselves. Try it today.

In order to become one with our Source and heal our deep rooted wounds, we must peel back the layers of our emotional "onion." The following pages will reveal a powerful exercise to assist in releasing these negative emotions.

Please take time to record this exercise on tape and play it back to yourself. Your unconscious mind, as I have said in other books, loves the sound of your own voice.

The first emotion we will release is anger, followed by fear.. Because so many people have anger stored up from past lifetimes, it can explode like a time bomb and must be the first thing you dismantle on your path to peace.

When I say we will also release fear, I am defining fear as anything that is the opposite of love.

Any state of being in which you are not fully connected with the loving peaceful hand of God is fear.

So let's get ready to do this first exercise. You will be so happy you did! And remember that because we have lived so many lives, you will want to replay this over and over again to heal at deeper and deeper levels. You cannot expect to regress back to the beginning of time on the first or second try. I know I couldn't do that, myself. This is a process you will want to repeat several times to get profound levels of deep emotional healing.

EXERCISE

Find a comfortable place to sit with your hands resting in your lap and your legs uncrossed and feet flat on the floor. If you need to, get a little pillow to put behind your head.

Close your eyes and begin to breathe. Go ahead and take a deep breath in through your nose, and exhale through your mouth. Again, in through the nose, and exhale out the mouth. Good.

Now begin to imagine a beam of white light coming down and in through the top of your head. Allow the light to move into your face, your cheekbones, your chin, into your neck, moving down the neck into the shoulders, moving down your arms into your elbows and down into your hands and fingers. Good.

Now continue to imagine the white light moving down your spine, one vertebrae at a time - slowly, slowly, through your back, your chest, your stomach. Relax. Relax. Allow the light to carry away any tensions and concerns you have and gently move them down, down, down.

Imagine the white light moving into your legs - into your thighs, your knees, your calves,

*your ankles, into your toes and into the soles of
your feet. Imagine the light becoming stronger
and stronger, moving through you almost like a
waterfall, just carrying away any tensions and
concerns you have and moving them down and
out the soles of your feet and down into the
earth.*

*Imagine the white light pouring out of
your heart, creating a ball of golden light that
surrounds your body by about three feet in all
directions. Feel the warm, peaceful feeling, just
floating around inside this golden ball of light,
knowing that inside this golden ball of light,
only that which is of your highest good can
come through. Inside the golden ball, you are
totally safe, secure and protected.*

*Feel yourself just floating inside the
golden light. Peacefully floating. Imagine that
you begin now to float higher and higher. Up,
up, up higher and higher until you find yourself
floating inside a cloud.*

*You feel so relaxed and peaceful here and
you are so high up in the air that you can now
look down. And as you look down you notice a
beam of laser light below you. And this beam of
light represents the way your soul sorts time.
Imagine you are floating over the current year.*

Chapter Eight

Now imagine you can turn and look toward the future and see how bright the future is. Now imagine you can turn and look toward the past. And as you look toward the past, are there any dark spots there? If so, go ahead and imagine a big broom is coming out and just sweeping away any dark spots that are there. Gently pushing them aside, imagine they are all gone right now. Good.

Now in a moment you are going to float back over this laser light beam, back over your past to the first time you ever experienced the emotion of anger.

Remember, you are surrounded by a golden ball of light, and inside this golden ball, only that which is of your highest good can come through. You are totally safe, secure and protected.

Imagine a beautiful angel is floating down right in front of you. Take her by the hand and imagine the two of you can float....back... over your laser light beam and allow the angel to take you back to the very first time you ever felt anger. Go way, way, way back.

Imagine when you get to the appropriate place that it will light up and you can hover over it. Imagine you are there right now. Good.

Now imagine that you and the angel can float down into this event. Notice what year it is. What's going on there? Imagine you are totally insulated from the event as if you are watching this on TV.

Allow your higher self to understand why you felt angry and notice that from this higher perspective, you can also now understand exactly why you feel that way and you get the lesson you were supposed to learn from it. Good.

Now imagine the angel spreads her wings and sends a blinding white loving light out into this event. See, feel and imagine the light filling the area and filling up everyone there with unconditional healing love and light. Stay there until this situation feels totally better. Imagine it is better right now. Good.

Now float up out of the event and slowly come back toward now, but only as quickly as you can notice that all events between that time and now are totally realigning themselves in light of this new decision and understanding.

Imagine the angel's wings bringing white light into every place in your laser beam, totally healing and releasing any anger.

Come back to now and float above now.

Chapter Eight

In a moment, the angel will take you back to the first time you ever felt fear. Go ahead and begin now to float. Gently float back over your laser beam and imagine you can arrive at the first time you ever felt fear. Imagine you are at that first time right now. Good.

Now hold the angel's hand, remembering that you are totally shielded and safe inside this beautiful golden ball of light. Begin now to float down into the event. What is going on? How do you feel? Who else is with you?

Imagine the angel opening her wings and spreading healing white light energy over this event. Feel the white light enter through the top of your head, moving down into your heart, down your spine, into your legs, filling your entire body with love and light and peace. Imagine the white light is like butter, just melting away all of your fear. Imagine the fear dripping off and feel it oozing down into the floor and going down, down, down into the earth. Good. Notice the fear is all gone right now. Good.

Now float up out of this event and take the angel's hand and slowly float back towards now, but only as quickly as you can allow all events between then and now to totally realign

*themselves with this new feeling of peace and
love. Allow the angel to open her wings and
spread love and peace throughout the entire
laser light beam as you slowly work your way
back toward now.*

*Imagine you are, once again, floating
above right now and go ahead and look once
more toward the future. Notice that this new
white light you added is almost like a wave, and
see how it moves into the future making the
future brighter than ever before. Good.*

*Now take the angel by the hand again
and float down, down, down back through the
clouds and back to the place where you started.
Thank her for being with you today and say
goodbye as she gently floats away.*

*Remember, you are still surrounded by a
golden ball of light, knowing that only that
which is of your highest good can come through.
Notice how much lighter you feel now and how
filled with love and peace you are right now.*

*Imagine a cord of brown light is now
coming in through the top of your head, it is
going down your spine and into your legs.
Imagine this brown cord going down, down,
down, and out the soles of your feet and into the
core of the Earth, anchoring and grounding you.*

Chapter Eight

In a moment, when I count backwards from five you will come back into the room feeling wide awake, refreshed, totally grounded, centered and balanced and better than you did before.

Five....slowly becoming aware of your body and the room, Four, feeling the chair against your back, Three, feeling awake, rejuvenated and refreshed, Two, grounded, centered and balanced, and One - back into the room!

How did that feel to you? Remember, you can do
this as often as you want because each time new
healing will occur! It is one of the best ways I
know to begin the balancing of the soul as we move
into a frequency of multidimensional healing. This
process and past-life regression healing helped me
to get energetic circulation in places where I never
had it before and I know it will help you too! Use
the space below to record your thoughts.

Notes

The Galactic Healing Process

Nine

Elemental Clearing

A big part of the Galactic Healing course deals with our understanding and eventual mastery of the elemental forces of the earth. This will become the foundation of your work from which all else is based, so we will be talking a lot about the elements in the next several chapters.

Before we get into discussing the elements individually, I want to talk to you about why it is important to learn about them in the first place.

After the tragic events of September 11, 2001, I found myself using this information exclusively on my clients and because of the extensive work I have done in this area, I know firsthand how important it is to balance the elements within.

Further, because we have lived many times before, we have perished in all sorts of ways, including as the result of the elements, or Mother Nature. I have worked with people who have severe phobias and traumas related to the elemental forces of nature that are initially outside their conscious awareness. They literally have no idea where the fear comes from - it is just there.

Once while I was working on a woman doing elemental healing work, she suddenly complained of being very hot and told me she could not breathe. I had just delivered the fire element to her and began to see a visual image of her soul trapped inside a barn in the 1700's. She reported seeing the same image almost exactly when I saw it myself.

I told her to imagine buckets of water pouring all over the barn, putting out the fire and that she should imagine a pure white light melting away her fear. Immediately, her body temperature went down and she calmed down.

This is an example of what I would call elemental karma. We all have it to a certain degree, it's just not always easy to pinpoint where and when it is going to show up.

Another time, a Galactic Healing student

had a similar experience shortly after the attunement into the elements. She also became overwhelmed, this time by the element of water. She had drowned in a previous life on a ship, as I am sure a lot of us have. Again, I worked to console her by having her imagine a life raft coming to her rescue and plenty of air to breathe.

It is for these reasons I have developed the next exercise. In this next part, you will be asked to go and meet with each element and heal any past karma you have together so you may free that part of your soul.

This process has worked for me, too. While leading a group through the meditation one hot summer, the group asked that the fan remain on and I realized I was feeling very uncomfortable about it. I told them I hate air blowing on me - in fact, I always had, ever since I can remember. For some reason, on this evening, it was particularly bothersome as I began to prepare for the meditation to heal the elements.

Sure enough, while we were in the process, I realized when we came to the air element that I had some unresolved past issues to deal with. I saw myself on a farm in the early 1800's being killed by a tornado. No wonder I hated the wind and air! It proved to be a very powerful healing.

Exercise

Find a quiet place to sit with your eyes closed, your feet flat on the floor and your hands resting uncrossed on your lap.

Begin to imagine a beam of pure white light coming down, in through the top of your head, moving down, down, down your spine relaxing you and carrying any tensions and concerns you may have down and out the soles of your feet and down into the earth. Good.

Now I want you to imagine you could begin to float. Just float, gently, peacefully, going higher and higher and higher into the clouds. Not a care in the world as you gently float, feeling totally relaxed and at peace.

Imagine as I count to ten you are getting more and more relaxed as you continue to float higher and higher and higher. Ready? One....two....three...four....feeling so relaxed.....five...six.....seven.....higher and higher...nine and ten.

So relaxed, so peaceful, you begin to notice a doorway in front of you. Go ahead and open the door and imagine you are stepping inside a beautiful room. Imagine there is a big comfortable chair and you can go right now and sit down there. Good! You also notice there is a big couch right across from you. It is so peaceful and relaxing. So relaxing.

Imagine there is a doorway at the back of the room and you notice it is opening now and out come the elements - earth, air, fire, water and spirit. You may not see them, you can imagine they are there and feel the energy of each one as they step inside the room and approach you. Imagine they are like balls of energy and imagine they say hello to you as they come over and sit down on the couch across from you. Good.

Now I want you to imagine first that the element of earth is there and that you could talk to earth and ask it if you have any healing that needs to be done. See what answer you get. Good. Now if there is anything you need to know about your relationship with earth, imagine it can tell you now. Good.

Imagine there is an energetic cord attaching you with earth. It is coming out of the middle of your body and connecting you with earth. Imagine this cord represents all past karma and past debts. Good.

Now imagine a beautiful angel has appeared and she is carrying a big sword or pair of scissors.

In a moment, when I count to five, the angel is going to cut the cord and free you and earth of any karmic debt so today can be a new day and all will be renewed. Ready? One, two, three, four, and five - see the angel as she cuts the cord and imagine a beam of pure white light pouring down from above, into the cut cord. Imagine the white light moving into your stomach, up, up, up, into your heart and head, arms and hands and down into your legs. Good.

Next, imagine you can talk to the element of air. Air element is there and imagine that you could talk to air and ask it if you have any healing that needs to be done. See what answer you get. Good. Now if there is anything you need to know about your relationship with air, imagine it can tell you now. Good.

Imagine there is an energetic cord attaching you with air. It is coming out of the middle of your body and connecting you with air. Imagine this cord represents all past karma and past debts. Good.

In a moment, when I count to five, the angel is going to cut the cord and free you and air of any karmic debt so today can be a new day and all will be renewed. Ready? One, two,

*three, four, and five - see the angel as she cuts
the cord and imagine a beam of pure white light
pouring down from above, into the cut cord.
Imagine the white light moving into your stomach, up, up, up, into your heart and head, arms
and hands and down into your legs. Good.*

*Next, imagine you can talk to the ele-
ment of fire. Fire is there and you can talk to
fire and ask it if you have any healing that needs
to be done. See what answer you get. Good.
Now if there is anything you need to know about
your relationship with fire, imagine it can tell
you now. Good.*

*Imagine there is an energetic cord
attaching you with fire. It is coming out of the
middle of your body and connecting you with
fire. Imagine this cord represents all past karma
and past debts. Good.*

*In a moment, when I count to five, the
angel is going to cut the cord and free you and
fire of any karmic debt so today can be a new
day and all will be renewed. Ready? One, two,
three, four, and five - see the angel as she cuts
the cord and imagine a beam of pure white light
pouring down from above, into the cut cord.
Imagine the white light moving into your stomach, up, up, up, into your heart and head, arms*

and hands and down into your legs. Good.

*Next, imagine the element of water.
Good. Water is there and you can now talk to
water and ask it if you have any healing that
needs to be done. See what answer you get.
Good. Now if there is anything you need to
know about your relationship with water, imagine it can tell you now. Good.*

*Imagine there is an energetic cord
attaching you with water. It is coming out of the
middle of your body and connecting you with
water. Imagine this cord represents all past
karma and past debts. Good.*

*In a moment, when I count to five, the
angel is going to cut the cord and free you and
water of any karmic debt so today can be a new
day and all will be renewed. Ready? One, two,
three, four, and five - see the angel as she cuts
the cord and imagine a beam of pure white light
pouring down from above, into the cut cord.
Imagine the white light moving into your stomach, up, up, up, into your heart and head, arms
and hands and down into your legs. Good.*

*The last element you will speak to today
is spirit, or akasha. Akasha is there and you can
talk to it and ask it if you have any healing that
needs to be done. See what answer you get.*

*Good. Now if there is anything you need to
know about your relationship with spirit, imagine it can tell you now. Good.*

*Imagine there is an energetic cord
attaching you with akasha. It is coming out of
the middle of your body and connecting you
with spirit. Imagine this cord represents all past
karma and past debts. Good.*

*In a moment, when I count to five, the
angel is going to cut the cord and free you and
spirit of any karmic debt so today can be a new
day and all will be renewed. Ready? One, two,
three, four, and five - see the angel as she cuts
the cord and imagine a beam of pure white light
pouring down from above, into the cut cord.
Imagine the white light moving into your stomach, up, up, up, into your heart and head, arms
and hands and down into your legs. Good.*

*Now that you have talked to each of the
five elements today, imagine you can ask them
now if there is anything else you need to know
today. Good. Now imagine you can continue to
receive information and healing in your dream
state. Good.*

*Thank each of the elements and the
angel for being here today to help you. Imagine
they all get up and walk back through the door*

they came in.

Now imagine you can stand up and walk back toward the door you first came in through. Now, you will find yourself floating once more in the beautiful, peaceful clouds, not a care in the world, feeling lighter and more peaceful than ever before.

Begin to float down, down, down until you find yourself back where we started. Imagine a cord of brown light coming in through the top of your head, moving down, down, down into the soles of your feet and moving down into the earth. Good.

In a moment, when I count back from five, you will come back into the room feeling wide awake, relaxed, refreshed and better than you did before. Five...four... three...grounded, centered, balanced...two...one...and back.

So how did you like this process? Use the space on the following page to record any thoughts, feelings or insights you gained from this journey.

Next, you will experience each of the elements individually as we begin to gain deeper understanding of how they may be of service to us in healing.

Chapter Nine

Notes on your journey to meet the elements:

Ten

The Elements

Next, we will explore the five elements and how they affect your being.

In the Galactic Healing course, you will receive an attunement and learn to channel and work with each of the five elements: air, earth, fire, water, and akasha or spirit, and learn how to bring all of them into perfect balance.

In order to understand our vast universe, we must first familiarize ourselves with the elemental forces of our own planet.

Chapter Ten

AIR
Color: Baby Blue
Season: Spring
Direction: East

Usually when we talk about elements, we say "earth, air, fire and water." It seems to just roll off the tongue. In healing work, though, you will use the air element first before the others. Air gets things moving. It removes blockages and brings people up, out of the doldrums.

When clients come in to see me for energy work, the sessions last an hour. Usually, unless I am intuitively guided otherwise, I have them lay on the massage table face up first. I begin at the root chakra and send them the air symbol, which you will learn in your training. I imagine air blowing on them from the root to the crown chakra, moving up the body and releasing any energetic blocks they may have.

Sometimes you will have a client with a lot of air in their astrological chart and they may not need much air, but usually I find that if people are coming in to see me, they are stressed out and feel the perceived heavy burdens of the world around them. Air lightens and makes them feel connected to Source and they can mentally check out and move into a relaxed state for awhile, which is a relief.

Air rules our mental plane - our intellect, wisdom and clarity. It signifies purity and movement and acts as the mediator between fire and water.

When you use air in healing, it creates a feeling of gentle floating. Air controls our respiratory system, circulation and heart.

When you are out of balance and have too much air, you will be hungry; if you have too little you will feel dull and heavy.

Society loves to poke fun at people with excessive air, calling them "airheads," yet the state of being you want to initially create for someone who is coming for healing is one of a more air-headed state, because they will be able to forget their troubles and you will be able to get the energy moving so they can receive a profound healing.

EARTH
Color: Brown
Season: Winter
Direction: North

Many times on the spiritual path, you will see people frantically striving to open their third eyes and crown centers, while forgetting to stay grounded in the reality we agreed to when we came to this planet.

Earth allows you to manifest your desires on the physical plane. Monetary abundance, creative or artistic expressions and childbirth are all a result of grounding on the earth plane.

Earth energy is stable and helps us to slow down and be patient and dependable, to endure under any circumstances. It creates density, and gravity and produces the interaction of fire, air, and water.

If you have too much earth energy, you will

feel tired and sluggish; too little you will feel un-grounded and non-centered.

In healing work, the element of earth is of paramount importance. After working with many clients through the years, I have found grounding people after energy work is one of, if not the most important thing I can tell you to do for people.

In the early years, I did not understand this and I began to get calls from people telling me they had trouble finding their way back out to the highway after leaving my office. Since the highway is less than a mile away, I began to realize they were not grounded.

It was not even that I was neglecting the grounding process entirely, but I was clearly not doing it to the level it needed to be done.

After events of September 11, 2001, I particularly noticed this to be a center issue of my work. People would come in for healing because there was so much pain and suffering surrounding that event, that I began to verbally walk them through a process to help ground them. This is something I now do with every single client and group I work with.

The planetary vibrational frequencies are increasing daily as magnetic frequencies around the earth are decreasing, as Gregg Braden reported in his work *Awakening to Zero Point*. Because of this, many of us are having challenges staying centered and adjusting to these dramatic shifts.

Here is a little process you can use to ground yourself and others in healing:

Imagine a cord of brown light coming in through the top of your head. Feel it, see it or imagine it moving slowly down your spine, between your shoulder blades to the base of your spine.

Imagine it splitting off and going down your legs, through your thighs, knees, calves and down into the soles of your feet.

Imagine you are growing roots from your feet and they are connecting you with Mother Earth.

Take all energy you need to feel grounded, centered, and balanced and allow any excess energy you do not need to begin now to travel down this brown cord of light and go down, down, down, into the earth, as if you are sending healing, loving energies into Mother Earth.

Now open your eyes, feeling grounded centered and balanced!

After you take your class, you will receive the healing symbols for each of the elements and during this grounding exercise you will also be able to visualize the earth symbol traveling through your chakras, giving you a further feeling of being grounded.

Earth occasionally comes up in the elemental clearing process.

One woman said during the meditation and clearing process she felt a deep sense of sorrow surrounding the earth element because she could feel the sadness and grief of her family members as they buried her in many lifetimes.

Here is what she told me:

"I was surprised to see that I had unhealed karma with the earth because I am always so big about being responsible when it comes to environmental issues and I tell people to love the earth and all of that. I had no idea I had so much negativity built up around earth. I feel bad that I didn't realize it before, but I am happy I cleared it up now! When I cut the cord with the earth, it was like so much sadness just poured out of my body I didn't know I had before. It was awesome!"

FIRE
Color: Red
Season: Summer
Direction: South

Fire is the masculine yang energy - the opposite of water. It is a destroyer, a cleanser, a purifier.

It is an aggressive element representing light, heat, expansion, passion, force and willpower. If you have too much you'll be thirsty. Ulcers, fevers, and some infections could indicate too much fire. Digestion is deeply affected by this element. If fire is suppressed, you may suffer from lack of motivation, inability to take action or covert hostility.

Fire is excellent for swiftly shifting energy to prepare for change, and should be used sparingly in healing. You can really burn people with it, so less is usually more. It should be used to get something moving that is really stuck - so stuck that the air element is really not enough. It can also be used to treat bronchial infections where the lungs are sore from coughing and the phlegm from the lungs needs to be dried out.

I once worked on a man who I felt was extremely shy - almost painfully so. I felt he had a lot of earth in his astrological chart and that he could use a little "spice in his life," so I was guided to send him quite a bit of fire - more than I would ever normally use.

The next time I saw him, he seemed to be more energetic and told me the energy work was powerful and had really made a difference for him. I did not share with him that I was using the fire element, although I continued to be guided to do so, and each time I saw him, he would become increasingly more confident and energetic.

Although fire should be used sparingly in most cases, it can be just what someone needs to "put a fire under them."

Always follow your inner guidance, above all.

WATER
Color: Deep Blue
Season: Autumn
Direction: West

Water is the element of the emotions and healing. It is the feminine yin that opposes the masculine yang of fire. Love, eternal life and the moon are all symbols of water. If a client is in need of deep healing after air is used for clearing, I always turn to water.

The salt water from the ocean is excellent for healing just about any condition. I talk in other books about the power of salt and the fact that no negativity can penetrate it. That, combined with the peaceful blue hues of water, is excellent for healing deep emotional traumas as well as physical ailments.

119

Water is cold and causes shrinkage so it is helpful for conditions where swelling is prevalent.

Water rules the glandular system and sexual organs. When it is suppressed, you may feel a lack of tenderness; excess can cause jealousy.

I want to remind you again that water is always used to heal very deep emotional scarring.

One student was on the table as I was demonstrating the elemental balancing technique and I was guided to send her a lot of water around her heart.

You will find this a lot if someone has deep heart healing to do. Water, particularly if you visualize ocean water, is really healing to our hearts.

In this case, the healing caused an opening in which she began to recall a past life as a nun. She was frightened and lonely because she was kept in isolation and prayer much of the time. The healing water was cleansing to her soul and helped her to release the memory and heal.

It is one of the elements I use most often in my work.

AKASHA
Color: Purple or Black
Seasons: all and none
Directions: all and none

Akasha is another name for the Source, the all that is or I'O, (pronounced ee-oh) as Hawaiians call it. It is the fifth element. It represents outer space, the ethers, far away galaxies, the entire universe and the cosmos.

It is the place of pure potential where everything is balanced and all is possible. I think it is an important part of the elemental system to get into balance because when people feel disconnected from Source, they tend to become depressed, despondent and hopeless.

Reconnecting with Akasha in healing allows you to feel the source of divine love and get in touch with your creator. It is just as important as earth in the manifestation process in that it is in that special void where prayers are answered and all is possible.

One thing I have noticed when working with groups on elemental clearing is that we would like to think our past with spirit is totally free and clear, yet many times it is not.

People have deep rooted sorrow at having to separate from their Source to incarnate. It is almost like an abandonment issue of sorts. It is very interesting. The healing that takes place with Spirit is often a huge release with tears of remembrance, as if coming home to a place you loved so much and had almost forgotton.

One woman described her experience in this part of the elemental meditation and clearing process:

"I feel so much better now. I realized I had missed feeling so free and peaceful. I now remember what that is like and I will be able to recall that feeling now when I need it to help me get through tough times."

Chapter Ten

BALANCE

As you work with clients and on yourself, you will use symbols for each of the five elements and will also receive an attunement for a symbol that brings each element into total balance.

In class you will practice working on balancing these elements within yourself and each other and you will send specific elements to alleviate certain ailments. The next section in the book contains the chart that will act as your guide in this process.

After working on specific health and emotional issues with the elements, your ultimate goal at the end of each healing session will be to bring the client back into a state of perfect balance and harmony. This is best done with the balancing symbol you will work with. It sets your intent to bring harmony to self, others, and the universe.

It is profound what can be accomplished by simply mastering the work of the elements and recognizing which element is in lack or excess based on information you receive from your client. The following pages can act as your guide as you explore the world of the elements.

ELEMENTAL CHART

CONDITION	IMBALANCE	REQUI...
abdominal pain	earth	water, air
acne	fire	water
addictions	fire	earth, akasha
allergies	air, water	fire, earth
anxiety	fire, air	water, earth
anemia	air	earth
anorexia	air	earth
appetite excess	air	earth
appetite loss	earth	air
arthritis	water, earth	fire, water
asthma	earth	air
back pain	earth	air
blood pressure - high	earth, fire	air, water

Condition	Imbalance	Requi...
blood pressure -low	air	earth
bowels	water	air
bronchitis	water	fire, air
bruises	earth	air
bulimia	fire	water, air
burns	fire	water
cancer	water, earth	air, fire
cholesterol	earth	fire, air
circulation	earth	fire, air
colon	earth, fire	water, air
congestion - see bronchitis		
constipation	earth	fire, water
cramps - abdominal pain	fire, air	water, earth
depression	water	akasha, fire
diabetes	water, air	earth

CONDITION	IMBALANCE	REQUI
diarrhea	water	earth
dizziness	air	earth
earache	water	fire
fatigue	air, earth	fire
fever	fire	water
flu	water	fire
food poisoning	earth	air, water
gallstones	earth	air, fire
glands	earth, air, fire	water
gout	earth, water	fire, air
Heart		
- arteries clogged	earth	air, water, fire
- broken	any/all	akasha
- congestive	water	air, fire
Heartburn	fire	water

Galactic Healing

CONDITION	IMBALANCE	REQUI
headache	air	earth, fire
hemorroids	fire	water, earth
hunger	air	earth
hypoglycemia	air	earth
infections	fire	water
joints -stiff	water, earth	fire, water
kidneys	fire	water, air
lungs - see bronchitis		
memory loss	air	earth
rash	fire	water
sexual organs	air	water, earth
sore throat	fire	water
stomach ache	fire	earth
swelling -water retention	water	earth, fire

Eleven

The Galactic Frequency

In level two of the Galactic Healing program, after you have worked with and mastered the five elements and learned how to balance them, you will receive an attunement into the extremely powerful Galactic Frequencies.

You will learn some exciting techniques that are absolutely amazing. Let's get started on them.

Self Healing
Drawing off excess

Right after I came back from the tunnel of light I saw during my near-death experience, I began the process we will now discuss. I instinctively began to place my hand over a part of my body that was aching.

I would imagine my hand was like a suction cup and I was drawing off excess energy. It was as if my hand was attached to a tube that would carry away aches and pains up and through my arm, across my chest and down into my other arm.

I would have the opposite arm dangling off the side of my bed and after waiting a couple of minutes, I would begin to feel a rush of energy as if the pain or discomfort began traveling up my arm, through my body and out my opposite hand.

It felt as if the energy would literally drip off of my hands and fingertips and I would direct it to go into the floor. This is a very powerful process to use in self-healing and works within a few minutes.

I also soon discovered that when I was especially exhausted, the energy would automatically drain out of my left leg and I would then imagine it going through the bed, into the floor, and down into the earth.

A good way to imagine this is to see the excess energy as a sort of fertilizer or offering of healing energy to the earth, just like when you did the grounding exercise earlier in the book.

Then, in order to replace what I had just removed, I would create a tube of white light coming through my right leg and into my body. This tube filled my body with white light and healed me at a deep level.

In extremely rare occasions, this is a process I have used on clients. I had a woman who came in to my office with a severe migraine and I put my hands on her head and proceeded to draw the pain away from her.

You may have seen the film *The Green Mile* where the prisoner on death row puts his hands on people and then blows the illness out of his mouth as it turns into hundreds of flies. This process is similar, except I am moving it through my hands.

I have, on occasion, blown excess energies out of my mouth, similar to what happened in *The Green Mile*, but I didn't see any flies, thank God!

If and when you do this process to yourself or others, you must be aware to completely draw the energy through your hand until it is all passed through. It is like a garden hose that you have in your yard. When you turn the water on, it takes a minute for the water to run through the hose and out the end so you don't see the water at first, although you can feel it running. This is the same thing.

You will feel the energy move from the body and begin to slowly run up and out your other arm. At first, like a water hose, it is slow, but then it will eventually reach the other side and begin to pour out. When this happens, it will pick up momentum and begin to flow quickly.

It is important when doing this process, that you run it completely through until the end. You will eventually feel the energy taper off from the starting point. This will feel kind of like what would happen if you turned the hose off.

When you turn off a garden hose, just as it took awhile to get it going in the first place, it also takes a minute until all the water runs out and the drip stops completely. This is the same thing here.

When you feel the energy is not as strong, you will lift the hand from your body and allow the energy that is flowing to continue to run through your arm until you feel all of the energetic flow move out the opposite hand. Make sure to run it completely out.

I would recommend at first to only use this as a tool for self-healing. You will find it invaluable.

If you've ever had an experience where you went to bed and your entire body ached from the stress of the day, this process is great for alleviating that stress and putting in peaceful white healing light in its place.

You may be wondering why you would even want to take someone's pain from them like that, and if this process could harm you in any way, so I want to address this issue right now.

The answer is no. At first it might seem to be too much to do, but it is very similar to practices of many indigenous cultures, and mirrors the shamanic tradition I mentioned earlier in the book where the shaman would swallow poison and ingest things that would normally kill other people.

The idea is that which does not kill you makes you stronger. The Hawaiian kahunas would do that because they could not possibly help others if they had not built up their immune systems and spiritual protection to the highest degree. This process is similar.

When you engage healing someone by drawing off their pain or illness and pass it through you, it makes you stronger. During class, we will practice this process quite a bit so you can see how to pass it through yourself without taking it on.

I want you to use your intuition, though,

because like I said, this is normally a process reserved for self-healing only. I have only been guided to use it with others a few times. The primary reason for this is because, as I mentioned earlier, I believe we experience illness to grow and learn as souls. If we were well all the time and totally stress free, we would not have anything to learn here.

That is why you would rarely use this technique unless guided to do so because you are not here to learn lessons for other people or to take on their lessons.

Which brings up another good point. Healing is not supposed to drain you or make you tired. If it is draining to you, there is something wrong.

When you are truly connected to Source, the universal energy that is flowing through you to others is coming directly from God and you are merely a conduit for that energy.

The Stronger Hand

One thing you will want to practice while you study energy work is determining which hand is stronger in sending energy, and which hand seems to be the one receiving the energy from Source.

Most people have one hand that is stronger than the other. I do not want to say this is an absolute, though, because some of you will be totally balanced on both sides. Again, I am offering a generalization here, but you will know for yourself what is best for you.

As for me, I have noticed that my right hand seems to be the one that is connected to the universe - as if I have that hand up in the air bringing down energy and sending it out my left hand to do healings.

Energetically speaking, I can almost always feel a greater flow of the life force coming out of my left hand and going into the energetic field of the client.

One possible explanation for this is that usually the right hand is the masculine and the left is the feminine. As if the right hand goes out and gets the energy and brings it to the other to be used in healing.

You may find your right hand sending more energy to others than the left. There is no right or wrong here, we are all unique in this way. I want you to consciously notice this because I have found it to be the key to success in drawing off energy.

When I draw energy from myself, I usually put my right hand, or the gatherer, on the spot that needs healing and I hang my left hand over the bed or massage table I am laying on and I imagine the right hand drawing off the energy.

Similarly, when I work on others doing any kind of energy healing work, I always draw the energy from Source with my right hand, while sending that energy to people with the left.

When you begin to understand intuitively how this works for you as an individual, your healings can become even more powerful. The best way to do this is to be as unconscious about it as possible at first.

Just let go of expectations and do what comes naturally to you. Then go ahead and bring that method you feel best using into your conscious awareness.

I know this is easier said than done, but I really want you to try to relax and "check out," so to speak, when you do your healing work. Suspend your thoughts and allow your higher self and

guides to lead you to what is best for you. They
will show you how it is to be done and by stepping
out of your own way, so to speak, the highest levels
of healing can be attained.

Before we go on, I would like to share an
exercise with you that will help you to allow Spirit in
to assist and guide your healings.

Exercise

Find a comfortable place to sit. Begin to relax and imagine a beam of white light coming in through the top of your head, moving slowly down your body, relaxing and healing you, carrying away any tensions and concerns you have and moving them down and out the soles of your feet and into the earth.

Imagine the light pouring out of your heart, creating a golden ball of light that surrounds you by three feet in all directions. Know that inside this golden ball of light, only that which is of your highest good can come through. Notice how easy it is to go into a state of complete relaxation right now. Good.

Now imagine yourself feeling totally relaxed and at ease and begin to notice someone is approaching you. It is your higher self. You can see your higher self, feel its presence, or simply hear your higher self talk to you.

Imagine feeling the high vibrations from your higher self and allow that energy to come closer to you. Notice the closer it gets, the higher the frequency. Good.

Feel the warm, loving energy of your higher self as it approaches.

Now allow yourself to move out of the way as your higher self moves into your body. Pretend that you are just a bystander now and that your higher self is in charge. Notice the feeling of peace you now have as you allow your higher self to totally integrate with you now, knowing that you will always get what is for your highest good.

Take a moment and totally integrate with the energies of your higher self. When you are finished, remember the golden ball of light around you and imagine you can stay in this state always and especially any time you prepare to do a healing.

Allow your higher self to extend one of your hands toward the heavens and the other out in front of you. Notice which hand is above your head. That is your receiving hand. Notice which hand is in front of you. That is your sending hand - the one that will be strongest in sending healing energies to others.

Thank your higher self for being here today and allow the higher self to stay fully integrated with you now and always. Ask for a sign from your higher self that will tell you when it is trying to communicate with you. Is it a thought? A sound? A symbol that you will visualize in your mind's eye? Notice what you notice and feel what you feel. Good.

Now imagine the cord of brown light coming in through the top of your head, moving down your spine and into your legs and go ahead and take all of the energy you need to feel wide awake and refreshed, feeling better than you did before, but imagine excess energies moving into the brown light cord and going down, down, down, into the soles of your feet.

You are grounded, centered and balanced now and when I count back from five you will come back into the room feeling wide awake and better than ever before. Five...Four.... Totally connected to your higher self, Three... coming back, refreshed....Two...grounded, centered, balanced, One.... and back!

How do you feel now? Isn't it amazing to feel the energy of connecting to the highest part of yourself? You are always connected to that higher source of knowledge, yet now you can hear it, feel it, and follow it even better than before!

Next we will move into another interesting technique. Use the space below to record any insights you gained from the last exercise.

Notes

Twelve

Other Galactic Techniques

Psychic Surgery

Now that you are fully connected with your higher self, you are ready to go into an even more profound healing modality - psychic surgery.

Have you heard about healers from the Philippines? They do a form of healing most commonly known as psychic surgery where they supposedly reach inside people's bodies, removing all of the bad stuff, while rearranging and healing faulty organs and tissue.

It is extremely controversial because they put on quite a show using chicken organs and blood so they can convince the crowd that they actually performed a real surgery!

I do not believe in that part of the process, but I think a more accurate description of this tradition is similar to the healing method we will discuss next.

After being attuned to the Galactic Frequencies, I realized I suddenly seemed to have more control over my etheric body than ever before. You will remember from the earlier part of the book that the etheric body is the blueprint of perfection we talked about earlier. It is the hologram of you in perfect health.

Using these frequencies, I began actually putting my etheric hand inside people to heal them.

Working on organs, mending hearts, and connecting with people on such a deep and profound level really blew me away!

You will be able to do this as well, believe it or not. Again, I ask you to recall the movie the *Matrix Reloaded* when Neo goes back to save Trinity. She is about to die, and after he finally realizes he has full control over the matrix, he reaches inside her with his hand of light (or etheric hand) and pulls a bullet right out of her stomach.

Later, when she dies, he reaches inside her chest cavity with his etheric self to restart her heart, infusing it with light until it begins to beat again.

I must say I have never done or witnessed anything that dramatic, but I can tell you it is possible to really "feel" people's ailments and heal them using the method we will go into in the next exercise.

This is nothing more than consciously willing your etheric hand to move into the body for deep healing.

In the next exercise you will experience this for yourself firsthand.

Exercise

With a partner, have one of you lie down on the bed or massage table. Put your hand over them and close your eyes. Imagine you are Neo and you can extend your hand of light into a place on your partner's body that you perceive is in need of healing.

At first, this may seem like you are making it up, and that is perfect. Go ahead and just pretend you can feel your etheric hand reach out and pass through the other person's body.

In your mind's eye, "see" your hand going down inside the flesh. What organs are you dealing with? Allow yourself to accept the first thing that comes to your mind as truth. Good.

What is going on with the person? Allow your higher self to tune in and trust that you know all that there is to know about this situation. Remember, your higher self is in charge and always gives you the best and most accurate information available. Make the appropriate adjustments to your partner and then gently remove your etheric hand from their body. Ask what feelings they had during the process.

146

Chapter Twelve

Realigning the Chakras

The next thing we are going to touch on is a realignment of the chakra centers in the body. As I have worked with hundreds of people, doing all types of energy healing, I began to notice something that intrigued me.

I teach a gemstone healing class and during the workshop I teach people how to become aware of the energy centers even if they have never worked with them before. Visually, the best way I have found to do this is by using a pendulum.

A pendulum is a stone or point attached to a chain used for divination purposes. You can train your unconscious mind to use the pendulum to answer yes and no questions and the pendulum can also be used to detect energies, which is what we will be talking about here.

To review briefly what I said earlier, the seven chakra centers each vibrate to match the color frequencies found in a rainbow spectrum. When they are open and functioning properly, they are rotating like colored tornadoes.

When you run a pendulum over a person's auric field, you can easily see the chakras spinning and it will tell you which ones are more open than others based on the size of the pendulum's rotation.

As I began to pay attention to the spinning on many different people, I was intrigued when I saw something that nearly everyone had in common. The lower three chakras - root, sacral and solar plexus - always rotated in a clockwise direction. The upper four chakras - heart, throat, third eye and crown - all rotated in a counter clockwise direction.

I reported these findings briefly in my book *Gemstone Journeys*. Shortly after the book came out, a woman approached me at a tradeshow who told me that for some reason her guides were telling her to come and show me something.

In just a few minutes the woman totally realigned my chakras. She said that each chakra should be rotating in alternate directions. The clockwise rotation represents the masculine and direct forceful energy and the counter-clockwise represents the feminine or receptive energy.

The rotation should be alternating with male crowns and roots rotating in a clockwise direction and female being counter-clockwise on the crown and root chakra centers.

On the next page is a listing of how chakras are to be aligned for both women and men.

Women's Chakra Alignment

Crown	counter-clockwise
Third Eye	clockwise
Throat	counter-clockwise
Heart	clockwise
Solar Plexus	counter-clockwise
Sacral	clockwise
Root	counter-clockwise

Men's Chakra Alignment

Crown	clockwise
Third Eye	counter-clockwise
Throat	clockwise
Heart	counter-clockwise
Solar Plexus	clockwise
Sacral	counter-clockwise
Root	clockwise

I have done lots of experimenting with this new, more balanced configuration and feel it is important to realign ourselves like this. It brings a new state of balance to your being. It gives a peaceful sensation of being connected to earth and sky that I cannot describe.

This process of chakra alignment is noted in *The Chakra Handbook*:

"the chakras rotate either to the right (clockwise) or to the left, depending on sex, thus enabling the energies of man and woman to complement each other."

I spent some time analyzing why our chakras are currently out of alignment and I have come to a conclusion I feel is valid. In the collective consciousness, mankind usually operates as a whole in one of the major energy centers. When man was living in caves, his survival depended on hunting and we were most likely operating out of the root chakra center. Then we evolved to the sacral center, and most recently, we moved into the power materialism of the solar plexus area.

So perhaps our chakras are out of balance because our society is such a dominant aggressive one in which the dollar is often valued more than affairs of the heart. Yet we are now moving into a time where we are doing all we can to open our heart centers and so this may change.

I believe there needs to be balance, though, and this shifting of our chakra centers may actually help us evolve more quickly and bring light and energy from Source to the planet.

When the chakras spin opposite each other, they act almost like gears, moving us forward. The opposing directions form a figure eight, which is like an infinity sign representing the universe as a whole.

In the next exercise, you will have an opportunity to realign your chakras and gain this new sense of balance.

Exercise

Now that you have already identified which hand is your receiver and which is your sender, you are going to have a chance to put that knowledge to work.

For this exercise you will need a pendulum of some kind. If you do not have one, you can use a necklace with a pendant on it, or in a pinch, I have even used my car keys. Anything will work!

Put the pendulum in your receiving hand and your sending hand over your crown chakra. You will remember from the last exercise that your receiving hand was the one that was extended up toward the sky and the sending hand was the one extended out in front of your body. Ask your higher self to allow the pendulum to begin spinning in the direction of the crown chakra. Notice if it is clockwise, or counter-clockwise. As I mentioned before, in 99% of the people I have worked with, both men and women, the crown chakra is usually spinning counter-clockwise, so I would imagine yours will be also. If not though, that is fine!

If you are female and your pendulum tells you your crown is spinning counter-clock-

*wise, then that is great. Leave it as it is. If you
are a male, you will want to respin your crown
chakra so it is turning in the clockwise, masculine direction.*

*To do this, keep holding the hand over
the crown and ask your higher self to begin to
spin the crown chakra in the opposite direction.
It may take a few seconds or even a minute.
Just allow it to be whatever it is and wait until
you see the pendulum indicate that the crown
chakra is spinning in the clockwise direction.
You will use the spinning of the pendulum to
gauge when the chakra is realigned. The pendulum will begin to spin in the opposite direction of
what it was before.*

*Next, move to the third eye. You are
most likely to find this chakra spinning counter-
clockwise, which is fine if you are male. If you
are female, hold your sending hand over the
third eye and again, ask the higher self to spin it
in a clockwise direction. Wait until you see your
pendulum spinning in the new direction. Then
go on to the throat.*

*Continue down the body and move to
each chakra center and realign them according
to your sex. Remember: males' crown and root
are clockwise and females' crown and root are*

153

counter-clockwise. You may refer to the chart on the previous page to guide you through this process.

It will take a few minutes to make the change, but you will feel a totally new sense of alignment that will help you tremendously as we move into the Galactic Frequencies.

How do you feel after that process?
Record your thoughts in the space below.

Notes

The Importance of the Etheric Chakra System

I told you earlier it would be very important to understand the etheric chakra system when doing this work.

In levels three and above you will be learning very powerful star symbols.

Before I get into the nature of what they will do, I want to talk for a moment about symbols in healing and why they are important.

In many healing modalities, such as Reiki, symbols are used.

The symbol systems usually have a shroud of mystery behind them because it is within those symbols that the knowledge of the energy is stored.

What are symbols? Symbols are merely a tool for the unconscious mind. They are an easy way for your unconscious mind to store an idea and an intent for healing - a short cut.

For example, if I drew out a little heart, you would instantly think of certain things like love, or Valentine's Day, and you would immediately be able to call that symbol a heart. The symbol is a part of the collective consciousness. It is easy for us all to recognize.

Healing symbols are the same. Each system gives the meaning for the symbols used and they serve as a cue to your unconscious mind and a focal point for your intent.

All healing is about intent. That is why earlier I said it is important to see your client as totally healed and in perfect health because you will get what you ask for. The symbol is used to give a quick and instant cue to your unconscious mind as to what it is to do.

In the Galactic Healing program, I said that the elemental symbols and healing you will learn will be used primarily for healing the physical body and ailments. In levels three and above, you will receive powerful star symbols, and the intent behind those is more about healing and activating the etheric chakra system.

It is important for you to see how those chakras line up in relation to the physical body to help you have a visual cue as to how yours will be activated in the fourth level of the program.

Also i n upper levels of Galactic Healing, you will learn to activate these etheric chakras in others.

Next we will discuss the possible source of this energy.

Thirteen

Discovering my Guide at last

As I mentioned earlier in the book, I have
been talking to my guides for years, but a long time
ago I asked that I not see them because I thought I
would find that too distracting. In my third book,
Lifestream, I described seeing the apparition of my
deceased friend and how startled I was at the sight.
I suppose that experience has stuck with me
through the years, so now I prefer to not ever see
full form manifestations of spirits. I certainly don't
mind if they want to brush my face with their hands

or touch the top of my head, and I may occasionally see them out of the corner of my eye, but I have asked that type of thing be kept to a minimum. Because of that, my usual perceptions of spirits and guides are only in my mind's eye.

It took a few years until my Galactic guide finally visually identified herself. It happened just after *Origins of Huna* came out and I was on my way to the airport.

I got out of the car as a family member dropped me off and as soon as I shut the car door, I remembered I had forgotten to mention something. I opened the door again with my right hand and somehow it felt as though someone pushed my head from behind. I slammed the left side of my head with full force into the car door, knocking myself out for a minute. Of course, nobody, at least on the physical plane, pushed me into the door.

It was a very "strange" accident because normally I am not a clumsy person and I would've thought that if I was going to hit my head then it should've been on the right side, not the left because the door was closest to the right side of my head.

Though I cried out in total pain and shock after I came to, I went ahead and got on the plane. I was headed to North Carolina to see some friends and all weekend I felt sleepy and had probably suffered a mild concussion.

For some time after that, I did not feel quite right. I intuitively felt that I had been literally knocked off my etheric track, so to speak, as if my etheric body was no longer aligned with my physical body.

I am a big believer in self-healing, but sometimes we all need some help from others. I went to some very talented healers, including one who several people suggested I visit. She would go into trance and speak to people in a language of light, a language which people did not consciously understand, but one that the soul would understand. It was like speaking in tongues.

While I was in the session and she spoke over me, I could not understand with my literal mind what was being said, but intuitively, I knew she was telling me that I would be able to speak in these foreign languages just like her.

I thought this was silly, as I often do with these things at first, but after telling a friend about it who had been a member of the Pentecostal Church for many years, she shared with me that she was skilled in speaking in tongues. She told me if I wanted to try it, I should get the Bible out and practice reading Psalms aloud.

I did that for five nights with absolutely no luck. Frustrated, I remember slamming the Bible shut one evening and saying aloud, "Look, if the Holy Spirit wants to speak through me, then so be it!" Just then, I felt a lightning bolt type of energy shoot through my body and I began to gush out all sorts of sounds and languages I had never heard in my life.

I could not stop it from coming out, and it went on for several days, nonstop. There were as many as seven distinct languages that poured out of some unknown place in my soul. The process of just hearing the sounds was healing to me. I could not get enough, as if a floodgate had opened and the very depths of my being were revealed to me. As if my soul had been drowning under a deep sea and now for the first time it was able to come up for a breath of air.

I had to get as much out as I could in as short a time as possible, as if all of that information had to manifest itself for fear it may never have that chance again. I found myself driving around town in my car speaking in these foreign tongues.

While driving down the road, I called my former Pentecostal friend and told her to listen. She could not believe how quickly I had learned it and told me that her speaking was something she only did on occasion and that it was very private.

On the contrary, I knew that I would be sharing these languages with people in my practice. One of the most profound sessions I had was with a man who was a Russian immigrant. He had been severely beaten in this lifetime, nearly to death, by the Russian police and was nearly paralyzed. He was a regular client and one day while doing the energy session I felt compelled to tell him that I was about to speak to him and asked if it would be okay. He agreed and I found myself chanting over him while sending the Galactic energies.

He was amazed after the session and told me that he was Jewish and he recognized the language as ancient Hebrew. He said I was praying over him. He recognized hearing the same prayer in the Synagogue years earlier. I was surprised because, of course, I had never learned to speak Hebrew in this lifetime, and foreign languages had been a hard subject for me in school.

Eventually, the seven languages dropped down to only two. Occasionally, others will appear, but two are most prevalent. One is from some part of Africa and seems to come through from a man who is a shamanic-type figure, and the other is a woman who speaks a language similar to those spoken at the time of Christ.

On a book signing trip to New Mexico - my home state - I became very tired so I decided to stop just inside the New Mexico border to sleep at a rest area during the afternoon.

While I was sleeping, I saw a powerful vision of an alien in my mind's eye. It had big eyes like the ones you see in Roswell. A typical ET look, yet this one was female and was a bright electric blue. She looked friendly, and I knew I had actually been visited because of other spirit visions I have had through my third eye.

She looks like the alien you may have seen in the X-Men movies, the character played by Rebecca Stamos, but that character is scaly, while my blue lady is very smooth. Her skin is bright blue and has the texture of something like the suit Batman wore - kind of plastic-looking. You may have seen the Blue Man Group on tv. She is that color.

I was not frightened, but I was startled a bit. I woke up from my "nap" and looked around the parking lot, only to see a couple of other cars around and no spaceships, so I continued on the journey toward Santa Fe. While I was driving, I began my chanting in languages when the sounds suddenly shifted from earthlike language to that of high frequency tones. Some sounded strange - like a metal band blowing in a light breeze.

When I got to Santa Fe, I worked with many healers there and one of them said, "You know you have a blue lady standing behind you, don't you?"

Of course, still not seeing these things myself with my third dimensional eyes, I said, "Yes I was under that impression," and I told her about the story in the rest stop and gave her a demo of my strange new sounds. She helped me realize that this was no accident.

The frequencies coming through were important and would be used in healing in the future. It was a validation of what I already knew myself.

Since then, I have had the opportunity to do sound toning for large groups and it seems to bring on a very profound healing for those who experience it.

I have seen that there is a way to "tune in" to the frequency of a group as a whole, as well as individuals. Each person has a little bit of a different tone to them and likewise, a group as a whole will somehow combine their frequencies together to create a common tone. It is a very interesting phenomenon.

The practice of Transcendental Meditation is similar because the guru identifies the mantra, or tone, for each initiate and gives that to them in the initiation process. There is another school of thought that says you can actually use your own name as a mantra.

You know the old adage that people love to hear their name being spoken. It is true. I tried this and it works. It could be because your name was one of the first sounds you ever heard. It brings a feeling of inner peace and connectedness to your roots which can help you achieve an altered state of consciousness. In the next exercise, you will try this and see for yourself.

Exercise

Begin to say your name, slowly repeating it over and over. You may choose to speed up after a minute and once you reach a speed you enjoy, continue chanting your name aloud for at least a minute. Each day, see if you can go a minute longer until you reach at least five minutes.

What did it feel like? Were you able to relax? Record any thoughts in the space below.

Notes

Galactic Healing

In Galactic Healing, the frequency tones I
channel do not sound anything like your name, but I
am convinced they are a key part of the makeup of
your soul. Since the universe began with the sound
"OM," it would be easy to conclude that on some
level you also began with a sound and this tone may
link you to your universal roots.

During the Galactic Healing course, you will
be opened up to sound toning. It is an important
part of the work because you can use your own
special frequency to actually help raise the planetary
vibrations.

This activation will be discussed in greater
detail in later writings and classes.

Fourteen

Messages in the Stars

When this information first began coming to me, I was guided to gaze into the evening sky and saw messages in the stars in the form of symbols. In the upper levels of Galactic Healing, you will be attuned to these special and powerful symbols for healing.

While writing this book I was told my guide, who identified herself to me as Aileahna, would now for the first time speak to me through writing. I suppose I could've asked her to speak before now, however the time was not right and I really did not feel a need for it.

The same has always applied in my regression work. People are often surprised to know how few regressions I have actually had considering it is such a major part of my work. I have not had many because I consider regression to be a tool to be used for specific purposes and that this type of information should not be abused.

So at the time of this writing, I am at a place where I feel I need to verbally connect with my blue friend who I communicate with telepathically everyday.

I held a class recently where one of my students was intuitively guided to bring some books about aliens in with her. Since the class was on a different subject, she had no way of consciously knowing I was going to tell them about the Galactic Healing technique.

We looked at the books together after class, and there was a lot of fearful information in them about the aliens who are visiting us at this time.

Although I have always validated that my extraterrestrial guides are of the light, I wanted to have a real heart to heart conversation with Aileahna to get the whole story. Here's what transpired during our talk:

S -Aileahna, are you there? And is this your real name?

A -My name is Aileahna, as you have chosen to spell it. It is the closest thing you have to the name in your language.

S- Since I have not studied much about the physical features of beings such as yourself, I had been told you are from Sirius because of your skin color. Is that true? I was originally under the impression you were from the Pleiades, or that I was being contacted by Pleiadians.

A - I am from the star system Sirius and part of the Archangelic Healing group you have read about on your internet. We are here at this time to assist you in shifting your frequencies to the higher levels. We are of the light and are here to offer assistance in the planetary shifts that are taking place at this time.

S- What is all of the controversy about a battle going on within the alien races? Some books say you are here to take over the Earth, is that true?

*A -There is an intergalactic battleground form-
ing here, and yes, we are a part of it all. There
are beings who wish to keep you right where you
are, in darkness, and if that happens the result
will be less than desirable. So yes, we are here to
engage in a battle of sorts and for that reason
some may have misconstrued our intent.*

 *Our intent is pure. We are working now
with the Pleiadians. You are reading much
information about us -some good, some bad.
You must look inside yourself and know truth.
You will know we are here from and of the light
to assist mankind at this time. Remember the
saying of BEWARE FALSE PROPHETS and you
will know that some who choose to cast a
shadow over others at this time claiming to
show you who is BAD and who is GOOD are not
always of light themselves. Ask them if they are
of light and if their information is of light and
you will be able to discern truth.*

*S- So where am I from and what circumstances
brought me here?*

A- All I can say is that you are descended from

*the Pleiades and they are your family who watch
over you now. It was the Pleiadians who initially contacted you in Athens a couple years
ago and it is they who are still watching over
you and wanting you to succeed in all you do
here. You are from Pleiades, as you have
guessed. You earthlings are so ready to give
everything a label. You have to be a
"Starseed," or a "Walk-in" or any other host of
silly labels you put on things. I am not at liberty
to label what you are and how you have transpired. I choose not to label things in that
manner and for all souls' evolution they must
also avoid labels. You are a soul, a light being,
as are all who are in this mission with you. To
evolve to the oneness you must let go of labels
and prejudices and all else, which segregates
and separates and pits one against the other.*

S - What have you come here to teach?

*A - We all have different skill sets and talents to
draw upon and for the work you are doing with
Galactic Healing, you are engaged in our talents
because we are the masters of the sacred geometry and the archangelic realm.
I am here to assist you with transmitting fre-*

quencies both in healing and in sound that will shift the consciousness. We want to share with you some keys to sacred geometry that have been long lost from time Egyptian and are about to come back. You may continue to learn these symbols from us and you will continue to understand their meaning.

Meaning is not as important - the intent is what is powerful. We have to get this information to you and it is hard to do because you always have to have an explanation for everything. If we told you something would save your life, would you question it? If we told you as we have already that something is going to come in energetically to remove illness and disease, would you question it? We ask you to look in your heart and have faith. You have protected yourself these years and know light. You know truth, now allow truth to shine through. You can do nothing to stop truth and light from taking over the dark. Truth and light always win!

We must begin to move into the realm of oneness if this planet is to ultimately survive.

S- Hey! That sounds pretty doom and gloom to me!

A - No, I am not bringing doom and gloom to you I am merely stating fact that duality mentality will have to be shifted in order to ultimately evolve this planet. What can we do to get you out of this need to know and instead bring you into a state of feeling, heart-centeredness and inner knowingness?

The mind is your greatest gift and challenge because you think instead of feel. We must move into our heart centers in order to raise consciousness. You hear this over and over again, but when will you get it and internalize it and live it? It is not a competition to see who gets there first. It is a team effort and all are needed to be in a state of oneness now more than ever!

S- What about my sound toning and sound frequency language?

A -The language of light you have heard and the sound frequency language you now know to speak is a heart language. Yes, people cannot always handle it. They want to laugh, make fun or ridicule, but that is because they know not what else to do with it. The language that is non-language is powerful because it speaks only to the soul - to the part of you that is knowingness and not to the mind. It opens the heart and takes you out of your head. Everyone should be exposed to this language eventually because in this state of nonsense, as you want to label it, all bliss is found. There is everything and nothing all at once. You know the words I say are true.

S- What about love? How can we learn?

A - Love - what can we do to really get you to understand the meaning of that word? It is not always about a relationship between the dual parts of society - man and woman. Love is an energy field of pure consciousness that is all encompassing. It is the all that is, or the pure potential of everything. Again, humans think you are closed of the heart unless you are paired off with someone. Can you not understand that you are everything within yourself?

Yes, relationships are wonderful for you and you need support and companionship of other beings, but that does not have to mean the presence of one person - it could simply be the love and companionship of friends or groups of you who gather together to raise your consciousness. Love is in all forms and no form at all. You are the ones who keep putting a label on it as you do everything. You must open your heart centers and love the world, love the universe and to do that you must love yourself. Just be the love and all else will follow.

S- What exactly is the Galactic Healing doing?

A - We work to reactivate parts of your DNA and we work with the five inner-planetary chakras as well as activate parts of your brains that have been dormant for eons.

The Galactic Healing is one of the energies that will assist in awakening others who will have new pieces to the puzzle.

In sum: We are here to help you if you will allow it. All tools you have received are part of the grand plan to reawaken the planet at this time and it seems as if you are working hard to get this information out quickly, but now is the time! There is no time to waste! We must work together for the higher good of all.

Yes, we are battling to control the universe, if you will, because we have to take back what has been lost to us and relight the paths that have been darkened by misinformation.

You deserve your birthright of a fully functioning brain and activated DNA! You have a right to reclaim what is yours. If you are on the planet at this time, you are needed and you need to wake up and realize you are here at this time by choice and for a specific task. What is that task you are to do? Are you doing it? Perhaps it is not clear to you at this time.

We are working with you now to whisper gently in your ear or give you thoughts telepathically or feelings that will help you in this time. Please help us by quieting yourself at least once a day to receive this guidance. This is how we are helping you and when you attune to this energy you are receiving our help as well by allowing us to be in your presence to open you up for the shifts that are upon us now.

Your planet, your people need you to assist them in this transition and now is the time! Right now! You ask what can I do? How can I help? You help each time you follow your intuition and your guidance. There are no coincidences, that is true and your guides are working through you now to bring light to the planet. The only way we can get this information there is through you. It is your mission. It is your calling. Wake up and answer the call.

In love and universal respect and honor - Aileahna

That is a powerful message for us all. Are we indeed being visited by benevolent beings who are here to aid us in our planetary evolution? I believe we are. Are these beings here to help us save the world?

It seems like a daunting task to take on such a project as saving the planet, but if you don't, who will? Why not you! You are, after all, a mere microcosm of all that is and all that will be. The time is now to begin the process of transformation.

That which is the source of the sun
And of every power in the cosmos,
Beyond which
There is neither going nor coming,
Is the Self indeed.
For this Self is supreme!

- Katha Upanishad

Glossary

Afterlife - the place the soul will go after death.

Akasha - term meaning the all that is, the universe, God, the place from which all life and everything in the universe emanates.

Astral Body - the energetic layer closest to the physical body. Deals with the mundane aspects of the world and physical existence.

Astral Traveling - leaving one's body behind as the soul travels to other planes of existence that lie just beyond normal human perception.

Attunement - passing of energy from teacher to student to enable the student to perform certain modalities of healing work. The teacher will begin the activation by opening up the chakra centers to receive higher levels of energy. It is usually done in a ceremony.

Aura - one of the many terms for the field of energy around the physical body.

Auric Field - the energy field that emanates beyond the physical body.

Blueprint of Perfection - see etheric double Causal Body - the third of the energetic layers around the physical body. Causal is closest to the universe and is the layer associated with connection to God.

Chakras

> **Root** - red color frequency deals with issues of grounding and survival.

Chakras, continued

Sacral - orange color frequency deals with creativity, manifestation and sex.

Solar Plexus - yellow color frequency deals with personal power and courage.

Heart - green color frequency deals with the physical heart and love.

Throat -baby blue color frequency deals with communication and speaking truth.

Third Eye - indigo color frequency deals with spirituality and psychic ability.

Crown - violet or white color frequency connects us to God, Spirit, Source.

Channel - someone who is able to run energy through themself either to deliver messages or to send healing energy to others. Acting like a conduit for spiritual energy.

Channeling - the act of allowing a higher source of knowledge or wisdom to run through you either in

Chaneling, continued
healing or by delivering verbal messages.

Consciousness - awareness

Conscious Mind - the part of the mind that is
aware of current events and can occasionally draw
on and remember events of the past.

Dimensions - a measurement dealing with length,
width and depth in the theory of relativity. Speed,
for example, is length divided by time. In New Age
thinking, dimensions are described as planes of
consciousness outside our conscious awareness.
As if we are existing on a plane that vibrates at a
certain frequency level, the higher dimensions are
vibrating faster than we are and are therefore not
perceivable to us by the five senses. The theory
being that if we raised our vibrations high enough
through energy healing or other methods, we would
then be able to see, feel and touch the higher
dimensions of reality and could experience them
easily and effortlessly.

   Second - deals with lines and shapes

   Third - deals with space

Dimensions, continued

> **Fourth** - deals with time

> **Fifth-Eighth** - indescribable levels of consciousness

Elements - the four substances thought to comprise all physical matter - earth, air, fire and water, and the fifth element, akasha, or spirit is now also recognized because it is the spirit or universal life force that runs through and animates physical matter. Can also be seen as the forces of nature.

Elemental Karma - past life ties to various forces of nature that cause trauma or phobias in the current incarnation. Example: unreasonable fear of water indicates someone may have drowned in a previous lifetime.

Energy Work - working to alleviate the stresses of the physical world on the energy centers of the body by placing hands over a person's body with the intent of running energy to them and seeing their energy field expand.

Epsom Salt - magnesium sulfate salt historically

Epsom Salt , continued
used to alleviate pain from injuries to joints; can also be used to cleanse the energy centers around the body.

Etheric Chakra System - chakra system residing in the auric field above the head and below the feet.

    Silver - connects us with fourth dimension

    Gold - connects us with fifth dimension

    Copper - connects us with sixth dimension

    Platinum - connects us with seventh dimension

    Opalescent - connects us with eighth dimension

Etheric Double - hologram of your physical body that resides outside of you and represents how you would be if you were in a state of perfect health.

Exorcism - removing unwanted spirits from a person's energy field through the use of prayer and ceremony.

Glossary

Extraterrestrial - a being who comes from
another planet.

Fire - one of the five elements that comprises
physical matter.

Frequency - the number of periodic vibrations or
waves per unit of time usually represented in cycles
per second.

Galactic Frequencies - describes a fast moving
high vibrational frequency that connects our energy
centers with those of higher dimensions of reality.

Grace - a sense of what is right, a reasonable
amount of time to get a result.

Heart Chakra - see chakras

Higher Self - the all knowing part of your soul that
knows all you have done and all you will do. The
inner guidance that leads you to the best choices.

Hospice - a care unit for terminally ill, provides
counseling and support for families of terminally ill
people and helps the patient make a smooth
transition into death.

Huna - a spiritual system created by Max Freedom Long in the early 1900's based on teachings of ancient Hawaiians. Presupposes the idea that man has a conscious mind, unconscious mind and higher self and has processes designed to help people learn to work with all three.

Hypnosis - a state of consciousness where brain waves are slowed down past the normal waking state to allow profound healing, increased capacity for memory recall and inner peace.

Indigo Children - term used to describe the new children being born at this time who have bluish indigo auras, or energy fields. These children are said to have the ability to live in higher dimensions of reality and are here to aid the planet in higher vibration shifts that are going on at this time.

Kahuna - Hawaiian term for expert in any field, usually refers to the tribal priest.

Karma - the law of cause and effect. What you send out you get back.

Kundalini - in Eastern thought, this is the serpent-like energy residing at the base of the spine. When activated, it leads to enlightenment by forcefully opening all chakras at once and connecting people with the highest perception of the God force.

Life Force - another name for the energetic part of you that is most connected to God.

Linear Time - the concept we accept in the third dimension of reality that there is a past, a present or now, and a future yet to come, suggesting that time forms a line.

Love - a state of being where we feel totally peaceful and connected to all beings and everything in the universe. It is the reality of all there is and all that will be in the future. The only real state of existence.

Meditation - calming the mind for a period of time to go from waking consciousness into a slower brain wave state to receive enlightenment, inner peace and healing.

Mental Body - the second layer of the spiritual energetic system that deals with creativity and manifestation. Lies about six inches above the body.

Meridians - thousands of energetic lines running through the body which allow the life force to flow.

Pendulum - a stone or weight attached to a string or chain used for divination purposes and to serve as a visual cue to the unconscious mind. Allows the unconscious part of ourselves to communicate with our conscious mind.

Pleiadians - friendly beings from the seven star system known as the Pleiades, known as the Seven Sisters. The name Subaru also means Pleiades in Japanese.

Portal - a doorway into another dimension of reality that allows for beings to pass through to our world and allows us to pass through to other worlds.

Psychic Surgery - a process developed in the Philippines where healers place their hands inside someone's body in order to remove an ailment. There is much showmanship in this technique and in demonstrations people are witness to the illusion of blood and organs coming out as the healer convinces the crowd they actually pulled organs out of the person's body with no scarring.

Psychic Surgery, continued
In Galactic Healing it is the process of placing the energetic, or etheric hand into someone to cause healing.

Reiki - healing modality developed in the late 1800's by Dr. Mikao Usui of Japan. Uses universal energy and symbols to heal physical and emotional ailments. Usui received his enlightenment after fasting on a mountain for 21 days.

Root Chakra - see chakra

Sacral Chakra - see chakra

Salt - does not allow any negative energy to come through and is an excellent way to cleanse the energy fields of the body.

Second Dimension - see dimension

Shaman - a tribal priest capable of otherworldly powers and healing abilities.

Solar-Plexus Chakra - see chakra

Soul - the part of you that is connected to all that is and lives on beyond physical death.

Soul Contract - the idea that we prearranged to meet certain people and do certain things prior to being born. Implies that we came here to learn lessons and evolve spiritually.

Source - another term for the universe, God, the cosmic all that is.

Spirit Attachment - when a wandering soul becomes attached to someone's energy field and attempts to live off of their life force.

Spiritual Bodies - a concept describing the three primary energetic fields around the physical body.

> **Astral Body** - energetic field closest to the physical body deals with the physical world and existence.

> **Mental Body** - energetic field six inches from the body deals with manifestation and creativity.

Spiritual Bodies, continued

> **Causal Body** - energetic field beyond the physical body that connects us to the universal life force, or God.

Stress - state of disease or chaos that will eventually cause physical ailments and illness.

Subtle Energy System - see spiritual bodies
Symbols (for healing) - any drawing that represents a certain intent in healing. For example, a heart may represent love so when you see it, you instantly know what it means. It serves as a short cut and cue to your unconscious mind.

Third Dimension - see dimension

Third Eye Chakra - see chakra

Throat Chakra - see chakra

Time - the fourth dimension of reality, the concept of a past, present and future in the third dimension.

Trance - a state of hypnosis where brainwaves are slowed down and healing can occur.

Unconscious Mind - the part of the mind that is all knowing like a tape recorder can be rewound and played back in states of hypnosis to allow the person to recall things from the distant past as well as the future.

Vibrational Levels - see frequency.

Vibrational Medicine - the term used to describe any form of energy work in which a certain high vibration tool such as a crystal is placed in the energetic field of the body in order to raise the body's vibration, therefore removing energetic blockages and creating a state of healing.

Walk-In - the theory that some souls choose to leave physical life and allow another soul to walk-in and take over where they left off. Usually done by a soul who has a special gift that is needed by humanity to aid in shifting consciousness.

Bibliography

Abbott, Edwin. *Flatland.* New York, NY: Penguin Books, 1884, 1993.

Andrews, Shirley. *Atlantis: Insights From a Lost Civilization.* St. Paul, MN: Llewellyn Publications, 1997.

Andrews, Ted. *Animal Speak: The Spiritual & Magical Powers of Creatures Great and Small.* St. Paul, MN: Llewellyn Publications, 1993.

Andrews, Ted. *How to Heal with Color.* St. Paul, MN: Llewellyn Publications, 1993.

Andrews, Ted. *How to See and Read the Aura.* St. Paul, MN: Llewellyn Publications, 2001.

Angelo, Jack. *Spiritual Healing: Energy Medicine for Health and Well-Being.* Boston, MA: Element Books Limited, 1991.

Barclay, David. *UFO's The Final Answer: Ufology for the 21st Century.* London: Blandford, 1993.

Bible, King James Version.

Braden, Gregg. *Awakening to Zero Point The Video.* Bellvue,WA: Radio Bookstore Press, 1996.

Braden, Gregg. *The Isaiah Effect: Decoding the Lost Science of Prayer and Prophesy.* New York, NY: Three Rivers Press, 2000.

Budge, E.A. Wallis. *An Egyptian Hieroglyphic Dictionary Volume One.* New York: NY: Dover Publications, Inc., 1978.

Bibliography

Carey, Ken. *The Starseed Transmissions*. New York, NY: Harper San Francisco, 1982.

Carroll, Lee and Jan Tober. *The Indigo Children: The New Kids Have Arrived*. Carlsbad, CA: Hayhouse, 1999.

Chopra, Deepak. *Quantum Healing: Exploring the Frontiers of Mind/Body Medicine.* New York, NY: Bantam Books, 1989.

Chopra, Deepak. *The Seven Spiritual Laws of Success*. San Rafael, CA: New World Library Amber-Allen Publishing, 1993.

Cicero, Chic and Sandra Tabitha. *Self-Initiation into the Golden Dawn Tradition*. St. Paul, MN: Llewellyn Publications, 1998.

Cooper, J.D. *An Illustrated Encyclopaedia of Traditional Symbols*. London: Thames & Hudson Ltd. 1978.

Cotterell, Maurice. *The Tutankhamun Prophecies: The Sacred Secret of the Maya, Egyptians and Freemasons*. Rochester, VT: Bear & Company, 2001.

Cunningham, Scott. *Earth Air Fire and Water.* St. Paul, MN: Llewellyn Publications, 1991.

Davida, Michael Alexandra. *Dominus Satanas: The Other Son of God.* Boulder, CO: CLSM, Inc. 2002.

Doreal. *The Emerald Tablets of Thoth-The-Atlantean.* Sedalia, CO: Brotherhood of the White Temple, Inc. 1992.

Drury, Nevill. *Shamanism: An Introductory Guide to Living in Harmony with Nature.* Boston, MA: Element Books, 2000.

Gerber, Richard. *Vibrational Healing.* Santa Fe, NM: Bear & Company, 1988.

Hay, Louise L. *Heal Your Body: The Mental Causes for Physical Illness and the Metaphysical Way to Overcome Them.* Carlsbad, CA: Hay House, Inc., 1982.

James, Tad, and Wyatt Woodsmall. *Time Line Therapy: And the Basis of Personality.* Cupertino, CA: Meta Publications, 1988.

Bibliography

Jenkins, John Major. *Galactic Alignment: The Transformation of Consciousness According to Mayan, Egyptian & Vedic Traditions*. Rochester, VT: Bear & Company, 2002.

Lady Sheba. *The Book of Shadows*. St. Paul, MN: Llewellyn Publications, 2000.

Lewis, Brenda Ralph. *The Aztecs*. London: Sutton Publishing Ltd., 1999.

Marciniak, Barbara. *Bringers of the Dawn: Teachings from the Pleiadians*. Santa Fe, NM: 1992.

Melchizedek, Drunvalo. *The Ancient Secret of the Flower of Life: Volume One*. Flagstaff, AZ: Light Technology Publishing, 1990.

Myss, Carolyn. *Anatomy of the Spirit*. New York: NY: Three Rivers Press, 1996.

Myss Carolyn. *Sacred Contracts*. New York, NY: Harmony Books, 2001.

Nichols, Preston and Peter Moon. *The Pyramids of Montauk*. Westbury, NY: Sky Books, 1995.

Neihardt, John G. *Black Elk Speaks: Being the Life Story of a Holy Man of the Ogalala Sioux.* Lincoln, NE: Univeristy of Nebraska Press, 1932.

Peers, E. Allison. *Dark Night of the Soul: A Masterpiece in the Literature of Mysticism by St. John of the Cross.* New York, NY: Random House, 1959.

Ramer, Andrew. *Angel Answers: A Joyful Guide to Creating Heaven on Earth.* New York: NY: Pocket Books, 1995.

Rand, William Lee. *Reiki: The Healing Touch.* Southfield, MI: Vision Publications, 1998.

Schellhorn, G. Cope. *Extraterrestrials in Biblical Prophecy.* Madison, WI: Horus House Press, Inc., 1977.

Schiegl, Heinz. *Healing Magnetism.* York Beach, Maine: Samuel Weiser, Inc., 1987.

Sharamon, Shalila and Bodo J. Baginski. *The Chakra Handbook.* Wilmot, WI: Lotus Light Publications: 1991.

Sherwood, Keith. *Chakra Therapy*. St. Paul, MN: Llewellyn Publications, 1988.

Sitchin, Zecharia. *The 12th Planet*. New York, NY: Avon Books, 1976.

Stein, Diane. *Essential Reiki*. Freedom, CA: The Crossing Press, Inc. 1995.

Stone, Robert B., Ph.D. *The Secret Life of Your Cells*. Atglen, PA: Whitford Press, 1989.

Summers, Marshall Vian. *The Allies of Humanity: An Urgent Message About the Extraterrestrial Presence in the World Today*. Boulder, CO: New Knowledge Library, 2001.

Swerdlow, Stewart. *Montauk: The Alien Connection*. Westbury, NY: Sky Books, 1998.

Taylor, Terry Lynn. *Creating with the Angels: An Angel-Guided Journey into Creativity*. Tiburon, CA: HJ Kramer, Inc., 1993.

Thompson, Keith. *Angels and Aliens*. New York: NY: Fawcett Books, 1991.

Upczak, Patricia Rose. *Synchronicity Signs & Symbols*. Nederland, CO: Synchronicity Publishing, 2001.

Virtue, Doreen. *Healing with the Angels: How the Angels Can Assist You in Every Area of your Life*. Carlsbad, CA: Hay House, 1999.

Virtue, Doreen. *Messages From Your Angels: What Your Angels Want You to Know*. Carlsbad, CA: Hay House, 1999.

Wesselman, Hank. *The Journey to the Sacred Garden: A Guide to Traveling in the Spiritual Realms*. Carlsbad, CA: Hay House, 2003.

Wright, Machaelle Small. *MAP: The Co-Creative White Brotherhood Medical Assistance Program*. Warrenton, VA: Perelandra, Ltd., 1990.

Index

A